GOD'S
FREE-LANCERS

GOD'S
FREE-LANCERS

JAMES C. HEFLEY

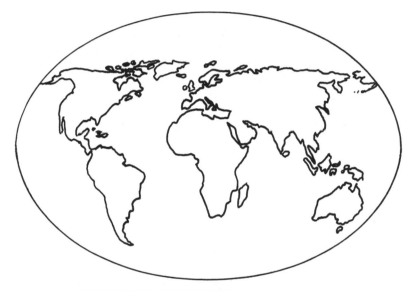

TYNDALE HOUSE PUBLISHERS, INC.
Wheaton, Illinois

Library of Congress Catalog Card Number 78-58745
ISBN 0-8423-1075-4, paper
Copyright © 1978 by Wycliffe Associates, Inc.,
Orange, California. All rights reserved.

First printing, October 1978
Printed in the United States of America.

DEDICATION

*No layman has meant more
to the cause of Bible translation in
modern times than Bill Nyman.
One of the four original incorporators of
Wycliffe Bible Translators, he served
as the organization's first
secretary-treasurer for many years.
While translators and support personnel
served in the steaming jungles
and remote mountain valleys, Bill Nyman
valiantly "held the ropes" at home.
To the memory of this beloved man,
who "being dead yet speaketh,"
this book is fondly dedicated.*

85726

APPRECIATION

Hundreds aided in the preparation of this book: past and present members of the Wycliffe Associates staff; leaders of Wycliffe Bible Translators, including founder William Cameron Townsend, executive vice-president Frank Robbins, and U.S. home director Clarence Church; Wycliffe field workers in Columbia and Ecuador, and JAARS personnel at Waxhaw, North Carolina; and many, many lay associates who gave hospitality and an abundance of interesting stories to the author.

Five volumes could easily have been written. So many inspiring stories were left out, so many dedicated associates went unmentioned, so many interesting interview transcripts were relegated to the files. The choosing was painful.

Where credit has not been properly expressed or where stories are incompletely told, I plead author's fallibility and beg readers' understanding.

It was never my purpose to glorify any single individual. I compiled and presented the stories of various associates to honor God and speed the Word to the remaining "unoccupied" villages where languages have yet to be written.

If by reading this book more lay people can catch the vision of service with Wycliffe Associates and Wycliffe Bible Translators, then all the toil will be amply repaid.

James C. Hefley
Signal Mountain, Tennessee

CONTENTS

INTRODUCTION

Wycliffe Bible Translators is the largest and fastest-growing missionary force in the world. Wycliffe's goal, seemingly impossible, is to translate the New Testament into every language on Planet Earth. Already linguists are working in over 600 languages, and surveys show there are still more than 2000 yet to go.

Outsiders are amazed at the fantastic growth of a missionary force that is avowedly nonsectarian and has no institutional or denominational backing.

Who is behind this group that has been lauded by *Time*, *Reader's Digest*, and *National Geographic*, and decorated by foreign universities and governments with their highest honors?

Wycliffe members say God. But then whom has God inspired to provide their personal financial support and give backup assistance for their many field projects?

The answer is a corps of remarkable lay people which is the admiration of other missions. This backup "line" of laity—not a precise definition, since Wycliffe members themselves hold the same classification—does much more than give money. Its members wire houses, ferry planes, install utility systems, survey land, type manuscripts, shelter missionaries on furlough, and perform scores of other tasks in assisting the "first line" of full-time field workers.

They are coordinated by Wycliffe Associates, the lay

division of Wycliffe Bible Translators, chartered to "harness the professional, educational, scientific, and technical skills" of ordinary Christians in the service of their Master.

God's Free-lancers tells how these "ordinary" servants of God have become extraordinary assistants to the translators who are taking God's eternal Word to Bibleless people in the most remote jungles and mountain valleys on earth.

ONE

UNCLE CAM'S ASSOCIATES

Before there was Wycliffe Associates, there was William Cameron Townsend. The founder of Wycliffe Bible Translators, who has such an audacious faith that he will never take no for an answer if God says go, began his mission work as a layman.

"Uncle Cam," as the octogenarian is affectionately known today, went to Guatemala to sell Spanish Bibles. There a young Cakchiquel named Francisco challenged him to translate the Scriptures so the 200,000 Cakchiquels could read God's Word in their own language.

Even though Cam had no theological or linguistic training, he determined to learn and analyze the difficult language so he could take on the task of translating. It took a decade of grueling, tedious labor and many personal trials before he completed the translation of the New Testament into Cakchiquel.

While living among the Cakchiquels, Cam and his first wife Elvira started a school, organized literacy classes, and even installed a power plant in one of the villages. Much of this was done without the benefit of previous experience. He just followed his God-given vision and forged ahead.

Cam learned of more Bibleless peoples in Guatemala and still others in Mexico. Before leaving California, he hadn't even known there were Indians outside North America. He saw that a team effort would be needed to reach all these linguistic groups, and he dreamed of an organization of trained linguist-translators who would take the Word to every kindred and tongue.

While working on the Cakchiquel translation, Cam was visited by a rough-and-ready evangelist named L. L. Legters. Legters quickly caught the vision and went off on a scouting trip to Brazil. He returned with the news that there were more languages in vast Amazonia than anyone could count. "I heard of only two that have even a portion of Scripture," he informed Cam excitedly.

The colorful Legters returned to the States to challenge audiences in his "deeper life" meetings to back the work of Bible translation with their prayers and financial support.

Cam realized that Legters was not missionary material; he could never stay in one place more than a few weeks. So the barnstorming evangelist became the first "associate," dividing his time between revivalism and serving as a field representative for the Pioneer Mission Agency, established to funnel funds to the translators and other worthy missionaries.

A. E. Forbes, a coffee manufacturer in St. Louis, might be called the second associate. He read about Cam and Elvira's work with the Cakchiquels and sent money for a turbine and coffee sheller. Cam helped the people form a coffee cooperative and Forbes' company bought all the beans they shelled. What did this have to do with Bible translation? By improving the economy, Cam helped keep the villagers healthy to read the translation he produced.

The great Christian surgeon, Dr. Howard A. Kelly, also became interested in Bible translation after reading a pamphlet. He planned a visit to the Cakchiquels but, after falling and breaking his leg, had to send a young doctor in his place. Cam kept in touch with the new medical associate and called on him at Johns Hopkins whenever he was in Baltimore. Dr. Kelly contributed to and boosted Bible translation for the next quarter century until his death in 1947. "Your great plan of searching out the language groups now locked up in inaccessible wildernesses and taking the gospel to them by hydro-airplane . . . will open up a new era in the history of missions," he predicted to Cam.

Cam had been thinking that a missionary air force might open up the remote areas of Amazonia to Bible translation. In the fall of 1926 he read a newspaper announcement that five U.S. Navy planes were to land in Guatemala City on a goodwill flight around South America. Cam was at the airport to meet the commander, Major Herbert Dargue, and outline his plan.

"My idea is to have a center in the jungle near a river or lake from which the planes would fly the translators in and out of their villages," Cam said. "We'd need mechanics and pilots, a supply of spare parts, and radio operators to keep in touch. How much do you think such a program would cost?"

Dargue was intrigued but couldn't say offhand. He promised, however, to "get together some facts and figures" and mail Cam a report.

A few months later Cam got a complete cost breakdown for a three-year operation. Three "flying boats" with pilots, mechanics, radiomen, medical personnel, and a hangar equipped with tools and parts would run $134,000, Dargue estimated.

Unprepared to act, Cam filed the information away in his mind. Twenty years later Dargue's proposal became the seed plot for Wycliffe's Jungle Aviation and Radio Service.

Cam's first short-term assistant was his nephew Ronald, whom Cam persuaded to take time off from college to help in literacy programs. The idea of short-term help wasn't new. Cam himself had first come to Guatemala as a short-termer. He never returned to college, but when Ronald finished his work he did go back.

After winding up his work among the Cakchiquels, Cam started the first training school for missionary linguists in history. Having only two and one-half students (one taught part time) for the first course held in an abandoned farmhouse (rented for $5 a month) didn't dampen Cam's enthusiasm. He simply scrounged around for help wherever he could get it. As in Guatemala, his only qualifications for associates were willingness and something to offer.

He found Amos Baker, an oil man from Oklahoma, fidgeting on a park bench in nearby Sulphur Springs. Baker, a widower, was waiting for his children to finish classes at a local boarding school.

After exchanging pleasantries, Baker asked about Cam's work. When Cam described the school and confided his plans for Bibleless groups, Baker remarked, "What a crazy idea."

Cam simply ignored the wry comment and asked Baker to help.

The oil man protested that he didn't have time and besides he wasn't even a Christian.

Refusing defeat, Cam promised to pray for Baker "until you accept the Lord."

A year later Cam was back for the second summer session of Camp Wycliffe. One of the first to greet him was Amos Baker, declaring that Cam's prayers had been answered and he was now eager to help.

Baker became the provisioner for "Camp Wycliffe," speaking in area churches and drumming up donations for the new crop of eager young linguists. He has remained a loyal promoter and supporter of Bible translation for over four decades.

Cam recruited many other associates to help out at the summer training school. Tom Haywood, a local hardware merchant, furnished nail kegs for seats and became a lifelong backer. Tom Trowbridge, a local carpenter, donated his skills and also gave money. Thirty years later Trowbridge was still active as an associate, doing carpentry work at the Peru center when past 80. Cam's aged father, Will Townsend, widowed and deaf, was camp cook.

In Cam's native Southern California, his most valuable

associate was an ex-lumber dealer from Chicago who had retired from business. Bill Nyman had already been sending the Townsends money. When Cam sent the first Camp Wycliffe students to California for phonetics study under Dr. E. L. McCreery at the Bible Institute of Los Angeles, Nyman offered the hospitality of a "prophet's chamber" over his garage.

The Nymans presumed the students had money to buy food for cooking in the tiny apartment. Nevertheless, the children, Bill Jr., Mary Ann, and Eleanor, gave fifty-five cents they had saved for a missionary offering. The students, almost penniless, used the money to buy white grapes, then selling for two cents a pound. After observing the grape eaters for several days, the Nyman children decided not to give them any more money. "All they'll do is buy grapes," Eleanor said.

Because of a heart attack Nyman, only forty-eight, had been instructed by his doctor to avoid strenuous activities, even climbing stairs. So Cam came to him. Whenever Cam was in the area he made the Nyman house his unofficial headquarters.

Not surprisingly, when the Bible translators organized, Nyman became the first secretary-treasurer. Single-handedly Bill ran the office and got the organization incorporated—all without salary. And when he retired after twenty-five years, it took five men to replace him. Defying his doctor's expectations, he lived to be seventy-six. His son Bill, Jr., became a Wycliffe member and his daughter Mary Ann became WA's first woman board member.

As others joined the force, Cam saw that a team effort was required. Cam's team concept went beyond the traditional missionary modus operandi—let the home folks pay and pray and let the missionaries go abroad and preach the gospel. Cam felt there was much more the home folks could do.

In a nutshell his strategy called for three "lines" of personnel.

First, the linguist-translators living in villages, learning and analyzing the languages, then putting Scripture, book by book, into the native tongues.

Second, the support workers—full-time career teachers, secretaries, medics, administrators, pilots, mechanics, agriculturists, government liaisons—backing up the translators.

Third, the homelanders supporting field personnel with money and prayer, providing hospitality for the members when home, and volunteering their work skills for short-term assignments.

Cam felt that completing the total missionary task would require the total cooperation of every concerned Christian. There would be differences only in function and relationships to necessary structure.

Cam's vision grew into dual organizations, each complementing the other. The Summer Institute of Linguistics (SIL) was incorporated in Mexico City in 1936 as a field committee responsible for overseeing linguistic analysis and translation of the Bible into minority languages. But SIL did not carry a Bible translation image to Christians at home. So in 1942 the twin was incorporated as Wycliffe Bible Translators (WBT). Interlocking directorates would make policy and keep the two working toward the common goal. SIL would handle training and contracts with foreign governments and universities; WBT would recruit members, receive funds, and provide information for home supporters.

Thus the "house" which Cam and his early colleagues built was a "duplex" with a common entrance. Then in 1948 the Jungle Aviation and Radio Service (JAARS) was set up to provide air transportation and communications. JAARS, with its own directors, responsible to the parent WBT/SIL, was commissioned to carry out special functions.

Cam personally directed Bible translation in Mexico, Wycliffe's first major field, for eleven years before leading a contingent to Peru. During his years of residence in Mexico he was constantly making trips home where he recruited scores of new "associates" who, for various reasons, did not go as full-time workers.

No college student was too green for Cam to consider as a short-termer. Two of his nieces came to help out. One, Evelyn Griset, later became a full member and married Kenneth Pike, who today heads up all academic training for Wycliffe and is regarded as one of the world's foremost linguists.

A special group was the Inter-American Brigade, composed of seven students who helped Mexican peasants with social projects. The Brigade was sort of a forerunner of the Peace Corps, except that the Mexican government paid them the wages of rural schoolteachers.

The older associates recruited by Cam to assist the expanding of Bible translation to Mexico's 100-plus language groups are too numerous for all to be mentioned. But two simply cannot be excluded.

Dawson Trotman was head of The Navigators, a ministry first founded to win American servicemen to Christ and train them to be spiritual reproducers. Cam and Daws became close friends, and at Daws' encouragement, many Navigators applied for Wycliffe membership. There got to be so many "Navs" in Bible translation that Trotman began telling young single women, "Join Wycliffe and marry a Navigator."

More colorful was the legendary A. M. Johnson, the wealthy insurance man who grubstaked a legendary gold prospector called Scotty and named a castle for him in Death Valley, California.

"Uncle Al," as the Wycliffe gang came to call him, was told by his pastor to look up Cam and Elvira on a trip to Mexico. He found them in the village of Tetelcingo where Cam was beginning translation of the New Testament into the local Aztec dialect.

Captivated and challenged, Al became one of the Townsends' most loyal and generous supporters. Cam completed his biography of Lazaro Cardenas while staying at the castle in Death Valley. Elvira died in Uncle Al's

Hollywood home. When Cam remarried, Al bought Cam's suit and the wedding rings, and gave up his hotel room for the nuptial night. When Al died, his will provided for regular payments to a "Director's Fund" for Cam to use on special projects. Though Johnson never became an official Wycliffe member, he played a key associate's role in many of Cam's projects.

After Wycliffe entered South America—first Peru, then Ecuador, Bolivia, Brazil, Colombia, and Surinam—the need for associates with specific skills and special funds became much greater. Cam sought key people whom he could count on in the United States. Most shared his evangelical faith; some did not. All had something special to give to Bible translation as associates. To mention a few:

Earl Miller, a California grocer with a hobby in aviation, heard Cam speak at a Baptist church in San Diego. "Cam's faith appealed to me," he said later. "For the first time I realized I could help give out the Word and become involved personally." Miller gave an airplane, became a key adviser in the development of Wycliffe's aviation program, and served on the WBT/SIL board of directors for many years.

Cornell Capa covered the epochal story of the Auca killing of five missionaries in Ecuador for *Life* magazine. Later he met Cam in Peru. From that day he became a friend of Cam's and a publicist of the work Cam held most dear. The bushy-haired professional photographer brought Wycliffe to a world audience.

Henry Parsons Crowell, son of the Quaker Oats magnate, played the key support role in the early development of Wycliffe's air and radio support arm.

Cam first called on Crowell when he was vice-president of Moody Bible Institute, and told him how technology was advancing the cause of Bible translation in Amazonia. Crowell was proud of Moody's missionary technical department which was training pilots and mechanics. When Cam invited him to Peru to see what Wycliffe was doing, Crowell promised to go and did. What he saw made him a lifelong supporter. Afterward, whenever Cam was raising money for a new building or another plane, Crowell was usually one of the first to respond with a sizable gift.

Crowell and many others among Cam's old-time associates have passed on to their reward. To replace them, Cam keeps recruiting others. After Maxey Jarman, founder of the Genesco Corporation, had made an unsuccessful run for political office, Cam challenged him. "You were willing to give four years to the governor's office in Tennessee, Maxey. Shouldn't you be willing to give at least a year to Bible translation?" The executive admitted he should.

Cam never stopped looking for associates. In Charlotte, North Carolina, he involved Henderson Belk of the famous merchandising family, and Frank Sherrill, then president of the S & W chain of cafeterias. In Florida he discovered Anthony and Sanna Rossi of orange juice fame. In Chicago he interested John Kraft, the cheese magnate. In Atlanta he buit a friendship with Fred and Grace Kinzer, known for their Kinzer's Salads.

He has drawn many, many more into the family of Wycliffe's associates.

Cam's associates are for the most part rugged individualists, eminently successful in their vocations, who respond to a personal challenge by one of their own kind.

Their overall contribution to Bible translation is vast.

TWO

LAUNCHING THE SHIP

Cam presumed that when something needed to be done to speed up Bible translation, God had someone, somewhere available to meet the need. And Cam had a way of finding the person who, as an Illinois advertising man put it, "could push the button." Whether it was a plane, a portable generator, a mural for Wycliffe's pavilion at the New York World's Fair, vaccines for an ethnic group threatened by a measles epidemic, or whatever, Cam could find the key man.

But as Wycliffe grew in membership and expanded from Mexico to South America, to Asia, to Australia, and to Africa, the "office" in Cam's inside coat pocket became inadequate to meet all the needs. Cam could only write so many letters, make so many trips, contact so many people while still keeping up with the field duties that his general directorship demanded.

And because of his time and energy limitations Cam was contacting only certain professionals, business entrepreneurs, and others who had something to offer. He could never reach the thousands of rank-and-file Christians at home who would help in practical ways if only they had handles to grasp.

Cam realized this and was trying to build up a network of Wycliffe lay representatives to show films, speak at missionary conferences, and help Wycliffe members on furlough. Besides Bill Nyman and a few others, he had very little help among the Wycliffe leaders. It wasn't that they weren't concerned; they were simply too occupied with their field tasks to be involved very much with the homeland. And hadn't the Lord said he would provide?

The lay representatives did an enormous amount of public relations work that many Wycliffe members were not aware of. But the rep system, as it developed, had limitations.

The men had full-time jobs and could usually work only on weekends. Most were not trained and didn't understand Wycliffe's policies well. And in some cities two or more claimed to represent Wycliffe without even knowing one another. The skeleton force at Wycliffe headquarters, then in Santa Ana, California, was kept busy straightening out schedule snafus and apologizing for slip-ups.

The representatives meant well. They worked hard. They felt Bible translation should be the first priority of the church. But because they were so far removed from the action, they had more zeal than knowledge and many Wycliffe members tended to be more critical than appreciative. For this reason and others there was a high turnover among the representatives.

One who never quit was a Greensboro contractor, Lawrence Routh. He suggested the Charlotte area for JAARS' international headquarters and enlisted influential lay people in the area to help. One of his friends, Melvin Graham (brother to Billy, the famous evangelist), chaired the construction committee.

Routh held banquets to promote and raise funds for JAARS and also aided Cam's notable airplane projects.

Cam would get airplanes by challenging Christian leaders in a city to give money for a plane needed on a Wycliffe field. The plane was then named for the donor city and a ceremony held at the local airport with a representative (usually the ambassador) from the recipient nation on hand to accept the plane for service in his country.

When the opportunity for a pavilion at the 1964-65 New York World's Fair came along, Cam asked Routh to help negotiate the building contract, then hold some fund-raising banquets to capitalize on interest stirred by the Fair project. The program was called "Operation 2000" in reference to Wycliffe's goal of translating the Scriptures into 2000 minority languages.

Wycliffe membership was now past 1600. To begin work in 2000 additional languages, over 8000 more full-time workers were needed. Cam was past seventy and soon to resign as general director. The far-flung lay representatives who came and went frequently were inadequately trained. Routh and the few others who had been working closely with Cam were on target, but they were unequal to the task.

Not being the mission extension of a denomination, Wycliffe had never had an organized constituency. Clearly the support base had to be widened to involve more Christians in the translation effort. And the lifeline between the fields and home had to be strengthened.

Wycliffe was structured well to meet field needs, but what about the home front? Should the membership get into public relations and fund raising in a big way?

Cam and a few others weren't sure this was the route to take. The most successful fund raising and promotion of the past had been done by individuals, mainly Cam's friends, acting mostly on their own. Wycliffe members were trained for linguistics, aviation, and other specialties, not for fund raising and public relations. And they followed the policy of trusting God to supply the need. How, some members argued, could you say you were depending on God while asking people to contribute? Cam, of course, didn't quite see it so strictly. It was one thing, Cam felt, to solicit for personal needs; it was something else to give out information on the costs of planes, printing equipment, computers, and typewriters.

One of those most concerned was Dale Kietzman, Wycliffe's newly appointed extension director for the United States. A native Hoosier, Dale had "laid his life open to the will of God" while a junior at Wheaton College. When he expressed an interest in missions, a missionary educator suggested he "find out" by taking the Summer Institute of Linguistics course which had recently been moved from Arkansas to the campus of the University of Oklahoma.

Cam was back from Peru and recruiting volunteers at SIL for the Amazonian jungles. But it was Ken Pike, who had also made a survey trip to Peru, who touched the nerve endings of the young Hoosier. "We've never worked in such jungles before," Pike said. "It's going to be rough on those going. One-third will be dead in two years. Another third will be invalids at home. And a third will continue working against obstacles." Dale signed up. He finished his schooling and went to Peru.

During his first four-year term he worked only fifteen months in a village. He spent the rest of his time showing people from different ethnic groups how to raise chickens, drafting legal papers for agreements with the Peruvian government, designing buildings, and repairing the JAARS airplane. Except for working on a farm and pumping gas for two weeks, he had had no professional training for any of these jobs.

Dale's brief stint in a jungle village had shown him the need for additional help. He, his wife Harriett, and baby Ruth were floating down a swift stream when their raft hurtled into a log, dumping them into the treacherous river. They were almost drowned.

Dale took over the extension job in the home office from Bill Wyatt, who had taken a leave of absence from his company to fill in. Bill was an old hand at representing Wycliffe and brought Dale up to date. He knew of about two hundred part-time representatives. They were an assorted lot—preachers and postmen, lawyers and carpenters. He guessed they were doing as well as they could, but the impressions they made for Wycliffe ranged from excellent to poor. Something had to be done for the sake of all concerned.

Dale agreed, but with a yearly operating budget of only $25,000 for home promotion and publicity of the work of

1600 field workers, he could do little more than pray and keep the mail current.

Furthermore, he realized that he and other Wycliffe members were fish out of water on the home front. There had to be someone else with the expertise and drive for building a stronger home support base. But who?

Dale prayed and asked people in the office for suggestions. "There's a guy named Butler who's been coming up here from San Diego," someone said. "He wants to start a lay organization to promote Wycliffe. We don't know how he'd fit in unless he took our training."

Dale smiled at the familiar line. It was held in Wycliffe that only those with training and experience in field assignments could effectively serve on the home front. Then they would get back to the field as soon as possible.

This didn't seem logical to Dale or in keeping with a longtime principle followed by Cameron Townsend that workers should understand and relate to the culture in which they lived. The frenetic, technological culture of the United States was drastically different from that of the minority peoples Wycliffe served. Someone steeped in the American way of getting things done would better relate to Americans than a Wycliffe member accustomed to the slow pace of the jungle.

Dale learned that Bill Butler had made several trips to the office. "If and when he comes back, I want to see him," he informed the receptionist. "Don't let him get away."

Four years before, Bill Butler had become a Christian through the shock of seeing a friend killed in a boating accident and the faithful witnessing of Paul Sutherland, his partner in the car leasing business. Bill had quickly become active in Paul's church, Scott Memorial Baptist, and also began promoting Campus Crusade for Christ in the area.

A lean five-foot-eleven, with piercing blue eyes, Bill was a fast thinker, talker, and mover. When Paul ran for the California state legislature, Bill served as his campaign manager. One day he was distributing handbills door to door when he happened to see the name WYCLIFFE BIBLE TRANSLATORS on a parked truck. Standing near the truck was a man with a crew cut. He thought he had seen him somewhere before. His memory suddenly clicked. Jack Kendall. The telephone engineer who had spoken at church about Bible translation. Bill walked over and introduced himself and recalled Jack's visit to the church.

A few days later Wycliffe pilot-mechanic Joe Girard, also a member of Scott Memorial Baptist, stopped by Bill's office. "What are you doing for the Lord?" he asked. Bill told him about his Campus Crusade work and his activity in Paul Sutherland's political campaign. "Why don't you do something for Wycliffe?" Joe challenged.

After they lost the election, Bill reflected on what Girard had said. He decided to drive up to Santa Ana, where the Wycliffe headquarters were then located, and offer his services.

The first two persons he met said they weren't the ones he should see. The third said Wycliffe didn't need a lay auxiliary. Then he met Dr. Rudolf Renfer, Wycliffe's stewardship consultant, who said, "I hear you want to do something for Wycliffe."

"Yes, I'd like to," Bill replied, "but I don't know if I can."

"Well, if you want to do something for us, find out something about us."

"How?" the determined Butler asked.

"You could start by visiting our jungle training camp in Mexico."

"How much and when?" Butler retorted. When Renfer gave him the answers, Bill went to the car where his wife Bettie was waiting and announced, "We're going to Jungle Camp." Her response was, "You're nuts."

Nevertheless, the Butlers went and were impressed by the grueling training for jungle living that the young recruits were undergoing. When they returned, Bill made another trip to Wycliffe headquarters.

Dale Kietzman was now on the scene. He set up a

meeting with Dr. Benjamin Elson (then Wycliffe's executive vice-president), Bill Wyatt, Danny O'Brien (editor of *Translation* magazine), Bill Butler, and Paul Sutherland, who had long been interested in Bible translation himself.

"Wycliffe is doing a good job on the field," Dale said. "We're getting more new recruits than any other Christian group and will soon have 2000 members. But our support base hasn't grown.

"We've had lots of lay people wanting to help, but they haven't been well-coordinated. What we really need is a lay organization of some kind that will hold the ropes at home for the members—pray, give, show films, provide hospitality when members are on furlough, and do whatever else our members aren't equipped to do."

Dale turned and looked at Bill. "Would you be interested in setting up this organization for us?"

Bill had just about given up and was too stunned to speak. "He wants you, Bill," Sutherland urged.

"I'll have to go home and talk to my wife and pray about it," Butler then said. "I'll call you next week."

When Bill explained that the lay organization was only an idea and that he would continue in his regular job for at least a few weeks, Bettie gave quick consent. Bill, Dale, and two old-time lay supporters, Bill Wyatt and Robert Bartholomew, began meeting regularly with Rudy Renfer and Ben Elson, who backed the organization from the beginning and interpreted its aims to Wycliffe members.

They looked at the operations of the Gideons and the Christian Businessmen's Committee. Neither seemed adaptable. They considered Cam's recent campaign to recruit 2000 businessmen who would help enlist and support workers for 2000 tribal groups. They studied Lawrence Routh's "Operation 2000" to pay off the burdensome World's Fair indebtedness (Routh had held fund-raising dinners across the country).

After many weeks of discussion they seemed to be getting nowhere. Finally, Dale abruptly announced one morning, "I make a motion that we move ahead."

"Do you mean that?" Bill asked hopefully.

"Yes, we're just talking ourselves to death. Let's move ahead on faith."

The meeting ended with no one quite sure what was coming. Dale went back to his office with doubts about what he had done. He became more worried the next Monday morning when he walked in and found Bill waiting. "Well, I've quit my job. Let's get going."

If they were going to have an organization, they needed a name. Dale suggested "The Lollards," after the lay supporters of the fourteenth-century English Bible translator John Wycliffe, for whom Wycliffe Bible Translators had been named. They felt that name was too unfamiliar. Then by a kind of consensus (no one remembers just who suggested the name) they settled on Wycliffe Associates. They decided the new organization should serve the purposes of Wycliffe Bible Translators, but not be just another department. "You need to have some independence," Dale told Bill, who was to head it up.

They now had a name, Wycliffe Associates, and a director, Bill Butler, but no money to set up an office and get the first projects rolling.

"Why not invite people interested in Bible translation to become members at, say, ten dollars per year," Bill suggested. "We could give them a specially designed pin and maybe organize them into chapters. Perhaps Wycliffe could make its mailing list of donors available." This was something that had never been considered, since Wycliffe guarded its mailing list and used it only to maintain contact with Wycliffe friends. Bill also suggested that other names could be gathered from lay representatives across the country. After careful consideration this was approved. But they still needed money for art design, printing, and mailing.

Paul Sutherland's father was a banker. Bill signed a 120-day signature note. Sutherland's bank agreed to loan $6,000 until membership payments started coming in, with $4,000 designated for the mail-out and $2,000 for Bill's living expenses. If the plan didn't work, it was agreed that Bill, Paul, and Wycliffe Bible Translators would each be responsible for $2,000.

About this time insurance executive Arthur DeMoss showed up. He had taken a couple of friends to Campus Crusade headquarters at Arrowhead Springs, east of Los Angeles, and they in turn had brought him to look the Wycliffe operation over. He was impressed that a Christian organization with almost two thousand field workers could operate out of an old church building and the second floor of a small office building. It wasn't hard for Bill Butler to convince him that he should help get the lay organization off the ground. Art's response was to assign his public relations expert, Gaylord Briley, to prepare the first mail-out.

As the mailing list grew longer, expenses mounted. By the time the mailing went out, Butler had spent the borrowed $6,000 and run up an indebtedness of $7,000 more. Almost everything was being spent on the mailing. He was spending very little for his own needs. Weeknights he slept on a cot in the WA office. He washed from a wash basin and cooked on a portable burner. Weekends he went home to San Diego to be with his wife and two teen-age boys.

Then the membership dues started coming in. When the bills came due Wycliffe Associates had $13,200 in the bank; and within ninety days, they had $50,000 in the treasury—proof that Wycliffe's many friends were eager to share the Bible translation task.

Wycliffe officials now offered Wycliffe Associates a charter and the green light to become a separate entity with a separate board. The first board members came from California.* Bill recalls: "I just asked who were the best guys to

---

*These first WA board members were: Dr. Rudolf Renfer (president for a brief time), James Beam, Dale Kietzman, Dr. Ben Elson, Joseph Profita, Lorin Griset, Paul Sutherland, Reynold Johnson, Everett Sweem, and Claes Wyckoff.

serve on the board and then I went out and buttonholed them and asked them to serve."

Bill moved his family up from San Diego. His wife Bettie came to the office as secretary, bookkeeper, and Girl Friday until she was joined by Sarah Pease. The first *Newsletter* (dated December 1967) was prepared and mailed to the membership. In it Rudy Renfer explained that the new organization had taken its name from the pioneer Bible translator, John Wycliffe, who:

> broke with a 1000-year tradition when he translated the Scriptures into the English of his day. God's Good News spread throughout England like a flame as Wycliffe's associates (Lollards) preached from and distributed handwritten pages of the Word in the language of the people.
>
> The modern Wycliffe translators have long needed an organized channel for harnessing the professional, educational, scientific, and technical skills of their many friends to assist them in their work on the field. Too often a highly trained translator has been removed from his assignment to supervise a printing plant, teach missionaries' children, build a bridge, manage an office, or do secretarial work.
>
> Wycliffe Associates are the modern "Lollards," Christians willing to place their God-given talents and resources at the disposal of today's translators.
>
> Wycliffe Associates is an officially constituted auxiliary of Wycliffe Bible Translators. Its operation will be self-sustaining, drawing no funds from the parent organization, but rather devoted to the development of interest in the total task of Bible translation.
>
> Issues of the Wycliffe Associates *Newsletter* will consistently feature the work of Bible translation and ways in which skills and resources can be matched to specific needs.

A sample of needs cited in the first *Newsletter*:

> An office building, printing office, and residences for Wycliffe's new headquarters in Australia on land donated by the Australian government.
> Pots, pans, utensils, and dishes for the Wycliffe group house in La Paz, Bolivia.
> Funds for printing newly translated Scripture for distribution to the Kekchi people in Guatemala.
> Beds, cribs, a small refrigerator, work tables, sandpiles for Wycliffe's preschool in Colombia.
> Five multispeed phonographs for class use at the school in Peru.

The January *Newsletter* announced an Associates car caravan tour to visit translators in Arizona and New Mexico. In March a call went out for construction workers to help build Wycliffe's new Alaska center just outside Fairbanks.

In May a list of urgently needed personnel was issued. Ecuador wanted a guest house hostess and a printer; Papua New Guinea, a printer; Mexico, a buyer, flight coordinator, bookkeeper, secretary, nursery helpers, telephone installer, and lay persons with other special skills.

The car caravan was organized. Money for supplies listed in the *Newsletter* came in. Volunteers signed up for the Alaska project; others applied for short-term service.

This was encouraging. But more money was needed for the larger projects. The Australia headquarters alone would cost an estimated $25,000.

They had to do more than send out a *Newsletter*.

THREE

FAITH PROMISES

The Lord gave Dale Kietzman the idea of holding "faith promise" dinners in restaurants for friends of Bible translation. Many evangelical churches had been financing their mission budgets by the faith promise method in which members promised to give above their regular offerings as God provided. If churches could do it, why couldn't Wycliffe Associates?

The plan had already been tried by the Reverend Lanson Ross, a pastor in Idaho. Ross had held dinners in eight towns and raised the money for a Wycliffe plane in Brazil. Then he had worked for awhile with Lawrence Routh in Operation 2000.

Ross was now working with King's Garden in Seattle, Washington. Dale and Bill flew up to see him. Their target was a plane needed in the Philippines. They had in mind holding faith promise dinners in major Oregon cities.

Ross suggested they offer complimentary tickets to Wycliffe friends in each town, then get local reservation secretaries to make follow-up calls before the dinners.

What about the program? One of them could preside, tell something about Wycliffe, then introduce the special speaker. Ross recommended Dr. Oswald Smith, father of the faith mission program in churches. Dr. Smith's Peoples Church in Toronto raised nearly half a million dollars each year through faith promises, and supported many Wycliffe workers. Bill called the Canadian pastor and secured his promise to speak. Then, armed with the Wycliffe mailing list for Oregon, Bill and Dale flew to Portland and rented a car.

They drove to the first town, got a supply of dimes, and set up headquarters in adjoining phone booths.

"I'm from Wycliffe Bible Translators," Dale told the woman who answered. "I'd like to. . . ."

"Oh, didn't I send you a check this month?"

Dale chuckled. "I'm not calling you about that," he quickly explained. "I'd like you to help us set up a Wycliffe dinner that will be held here in about three months." Then he gave more details and asked if she would serve as reservation secretary.

Dale and Bill kept calling until they got ten secretaries who would take tickets. Then they went on to the next town.

When they got back to Portland on the eighth day, Bill decided they'd been paying too much for motel rooms. "Let's look for a cheaper one tonight," he suggested. At the fourth stop, he got a quote of less than ten dollars a night and took the room sight unseen. It was on the back side of an old house. A clanging radiator was beside one wall and the two rickety beds looked as if they were ready for the junkyard. Dale was too tired to protest.

They returned to Santa Ana and had tickets and programs printed. Three months later Bill met Dr. Smith at the Portland airport. Moving from town to town, they averaged about $12,000 in cash and faith promises from each dinner. The plane was bought and dedicated in Portland with many of the donors present.

With some confidence Bill told Dale, "If it will work for eight dinners it will work for twenty, forty, or sixty. But I'll need another man." Dale and the other board members concurred.

Bill had taught a teenagers' Sunday school class at church before coming to Wycliffe Associates. He called the department director, Johnny Mitchell, an energetic young food broker in San Diego, about joining WA full time.

Johnny and his wife Mitzi would travel together, Bill pro-posed, enlisting lay people across the country in support of Wycliffe. After praying, Mitzi remarked, "We'd be taking a reduction in salary, but money shouldn't deter-mine God's will for our lives." In March 1969, Johnny became the first area director for Wycliffe Associates.

The Mitchells joined Bill on the second series of faith promise dinner meetings. At the third dinner, in Yuma, Arizona, Bill asked Johnny to emcee the program. After-ward Bill said, "You're on your own now, Johnny."

Wycliffe Associates scheduled over seventy faith prom-ise dinners in seventeen states for the fall of 1969. Seven Wycliffe missionaries (Herman Aschmann, Cecil Hawkins, Bernie May, Jim Wilson, Ken Jacobs, Hugh Steven, and John Waller), layman Jack Kendall, and Mexican Totonac co-translator Manuel Arenas comprised the speaking staff. Bernie May told how JAARS provided a supply lifeline to translators scattered across the previously unreachable jungles of Peru. Ken Jacobs described how the gospel had triumphed among the Chamula people in Mexico despite severe persecution.

Manuel Arenas recalled serving as Herman Aschmann's language helper in the Totonac mountain village. "I was just a little illiterate mountain boy who worshiped images when Herman found me," the intense dark-haired young Totonac said. "Today I have a Master's degree, speak six languages, and am directing a Bible school for my people."

But it was Jack Kendall, the rugged, rawboned telephone engineer, who drew the greatest response from men. "Wycliffe needs electricians, plumbers, telephone men, and other skilled workers for installing WET (water, elec-tric, and telephone) systems at Wycliffe centers. The trans-lators and other full-time Wycliffe workers shouldn't have to waste their time boiling water, repairing broken-down, worn-out generators, and running across the base to de-liver messages. Let's help them get on with their main job —giving God's Word to everyone in his own language." Everywhere he spoke, Kendall called for laymen to give

37

their talents and vacation time and pay their own expenses for work safaris to the fields. The dozens of men who responded were typified by an Ohio engineer who said, "All my life I've prayed and given money to missions. Now I have a chance to do something with my hands."

Guests at the dinner meetings were invited to make faith promises for specific projects. A unique computer system was the challenge for Wycliffe friends in Minneapolis-St. Paul, Minnesota, who promised $9,000 for that system plus $5,000 for the general support fund of Wycliffe.

The computer project was initiated when Dan Velie, translator for the Orejon people of Peru, returned home on furlough. Velie had heard from Wycliffe's Consultant in Computational Linguistics, Dr. Joe Grimes, about the use of computers in preparing manuscripts for the printer in Mexico. Dan and his father-in-law, the Reverend Leroy Cook, talked to Paul Ramseyer, manager of Radio KTIS and chairman of the local WA chapter, and Dan Moore, president of Tri-Data Corporation. They referred Dan to Carolyn Holden, a systems analyst at the Billy Graham Evangelistic Association in Minneapolis. The result was a computer system that would dramatically lessen the number of re-typings and proofreadings in preparing final Scripture manuscripts for printing.

Here's how it worked: on a typewriter the preliminary draft of a translation was typed and sent to the Graham headquarters in Minneapolis. There a Control Data 915 page-reader scanned the manuscript and stored the data on magnetic tape, which was then fed into a General Electric 425 computer. Necessary changes were typed by the translator, sent to Minneapolis, and fed into the original tape. Retyping and proofreading of the entire manuscript was never necessary, with the final version produced by the computer ready for the printer. Concordances and word lists were also created for dictionaries and further language analysis. Months, even years of tedious hand work by the translators on the field was saved.

More projects and another series of dinner meetings

were planned for the spring of 1970. In April alone 3387 persons promised $317,261 to help speed God's Word to Bibleless people around the world. The fall brought a single dinner record when over 500 attended at Knott's Berry Farm, Buena Park, California, and promised $18,000, part of which went to aid the victims of the terrible Peruvian earthquake. Before the dinner, Bill Butler and WA treasurer Rey Johnson had slipped into a closet and prayed for exactly that amount.

Spring and fall, year after year, the dinner series continued, with Wycliffe Associates staffers presiding and Wycliffe members usually speaking. Neil and Jane Nellis, who had spent over twenty-five years with the Sierra Juarez Zapoteco people of Mexico, brought two friends skilled with the blowgun. Each night one of the young men demonstrated his markmanship by shooting a small plastic doll from a table with a mudball. One evening while they were setting up the tables, Johnny Mitchell suggested, "Neil, if you really have confidence in this guy and want to be a hero, let him shoot the doll off your head." That night the translator stood about thirty feet away with his back to the Zapoteco. The young man puffed and blew. The doll went flying. But on another occasion, the Zapoteco aimed too low and shot the mudball into the bald spot on the back of Neil's head. The audience gasped, but Neil turned and grinned at the young man.

One day on the road Mitchell asked the Nellises, "What is something you've always wanted your people to have?" Jane, an accomplished musician, smiled. "We've dreamed of an orchestra, but could never afford to buy the instruments. If we had the instruments, we could teach the people to play."

At following dinners Mitchell mentioned their wish and invited people to donate old instruments "gathering dust" in their homes. The WA *Newsletter* also ran a brief announcement about the need. By the end of the tour the Nellises needed a trailer to haul back to Mexico all the guitars, clarinets, saxophones, accordions, and other instruments they had been given. Several months later they mailed a tape of the Zapoteco orchestra to Johnny Mitchell, suggesting he send copies to the donors. The first hymn the Zapotecos had learned was "A Mighty Fortress Is Our God."

One of the most impressive foreigners to tour a dinner circuit was Yapeta Tikepo, a converted Wiru witch doctor from the remote highlands of Papua New Guinea. Yapeta drew rapt attention when he gave his testimony. Someone asked him what had impressed him most about his visit to the United States with translator Dr. Harland Kerr. "Traveling on a California freeway and seeing an elephant in a zoo," he replied.

The biggest crowds came to hear Rachel Saint and three Auca Christians from Ecuador. Accompanied by WA staff members, they flew in a Cessna Skywagon, stopping for "Auca Update Rallies" in twenty-three cities. In several places the crowds were so great that an extra meeting had to be held. Back in California, WA office workers took fifteen-minute turns in a prayer closet while the Auca tour group was on the road.

At each rally an awe-inspiring multimedia film story of the killings and the work of Betty Elliot, Rachel Saint (sister to pilot Nate Saint), and Rachel's Wycliffe co-worker Dr. Catherine Peeke, was shown. Then, after the seven projectors had been turned off, Rachel presented the Aucas, noting that two had participated in spearing the missionaries in 1956.

The appearance of Rachel and the Aucas was a media event in every city they visited. Newspaper reporters and television crews vied for interviews. They appeared on the NBC-TV "Today Show," and *Esquire* magazine published a long article about the change among the Aucas. Never before had missionary work been so publicized in the United States.

The gifts received and spiritual decisions made at the rallies were evidence that Christians were deeply involved in missions and were there to encourage Rachel and welcome fellow Christians from another culture. Rachel and the Aucas received a standing ovation at the end of every rally. Thousands of Christians were visibly moved. Herbert Whealy, vice-chairman of Wycliffe's Canadian Home Council, confided his reaction at the Detroit rally: "When Rachel introduced Gikita as 'the one who speared my brother,' and as I heard his testimony, I cried like a baby." And Wallace McGehee, a manufacturer in Kansas City, declared, "Never have I witnessed any event that gave me such a spiritual uplift as did this rally.... It was like reading a letter from the Apostle Paul."

The Auca Update Rallies were a dramatic exception in the pattern of WA promotion. The faith promise dinners, which continue today, have been the primary means of raising money and enlisting volunteers for Wycliffe projects and attracting new Wycliffe supporters. On the average, 60 percent of those attending dinner meetings are new to Wycliffe.

The dinner schedule has been vastly expanded since the initial pilot project was launched in Oregon in 1969. In 1976, 297 dinners were held from Hawaii to New England and from Alaska to Florida. Total faith promises amounted to almost one million dollars. In 1977 another 300 faith promise dinners were scheduled.

It is no easy task to plan, coordinate, promote, and program 300 such dinners a year. The planning starts in vice-president Warren Nelson's office at WA headquarters in California. "It's a big job, but we've found a way to do it," he says. "Several years ago we started using the zip code areas. Every twelve to eighteen months we try to have one or more dinner meetings in each area."

Warren stands before a large U.S. wall map divided into territories, each handled by an area director. Colored map pins mark the sites for future dinners during the next year and a half. Green is for this spring, yellow for fall, and red for next spring.

"Right now [spring] we're looking toward the fall. We've already selected the cities where we plan to hold the dinners. Now we'll make a list of the zip codes in which the cities are located and ask Wycliffe Bible Translators for a computer list of friends who live in these areas. This becomes our mailing list.

"Take this place, for instance." Warren points to Cleveland, Tennessee, on the map. "Paul Chappell, our southeast area director, has trained three persons to serve as reservation secretaries. He always tries to get people from different churches and communities. Some of them will have worked on a previous dinner.

"Invitations are mailed out and the people are encouraged to make reservations for themselves and their friends by calling one of the reservation secretaries. Many call. The secretaries phone others as a follow-up to the invitation. Paul keeps in touch by phone."

The date of the Cleveland dinner arrives. We take the Highway 64 exit off Interstate 75 and drive into the parking lot of the local Holiday Inn where, weeks before, Paul made arrangements to have the dinner meeting. Several days ago he confirmed the number of reservations.

In the dining room tables are neatly arranged in banquet style, covered by gold cloths and with the place settings already on. Paul and the missionary speaker check in and then return to the car for equipment and books. Thirty minutes before time to start, the equipment is all in place and the missionary speaker is putting registration cards at each table setting. An interesting variety of Wycliffe books and literature have been arranged on a table beside the main door.

Dinner begins promptly at seven. Tonight the menu is fried chicken, baked potato, tossed salad, rolls, beverage, and dessert. Costs vary from state to state, and they keep climbing, but this one is $4.50 per meal.

When the guests have finished dessert, Paul rises from his chair to begin the program. At the speaker's stand he pushes a strand of yellow hair from his face, adjusts his tie, and offers a Jimmy Carter smile.

"I'm Paul Chappell, your host," he drawls. "Welcome to

the Wycliffe Associates dinner. One of our rules is to start the program at exactly eight o'clock, so if you'll just set your watches back a bit. . . ." Everyone laughs.

"We really praise the Lord for those who helped make this dinner possible. We especially appreciate those who called everyone so cheerfully. I remember phoning a young woman in Alabama to ask her help in taking reservations for a dinner. 'Wonderful,' she said. 'Last night I got on my knees and asked God to show me something to do. You answered my prayer.'

"You reservation secretaries are an answer to prayer. Will you please stand so I can introduce you."

After the secretaries are acknowledged with applause, Paul asks any members of the Wycliffe family to stand. David Turner, son of Glen and Jeannie Turner from Ecuador, is a student at nearby Bryan College. A woman stands behind him and introduces herself as the aunt of George Fletcher, a JAARS pilot in the Philippines.

Paul looks toward the Wycliffe speaker. "Many of you prayed for the Millers while they were held captive in Vietnam. Now, thank God, they're back with us, and tonight John is going to share some of their experiences."

The translator's gaunt face still shows the effects of the prison camps. But his voice is strong, as for the fourteenth time in the past eighteen days he speaks for a half hour about how God sustained him and his wife and daughter through eight months of imprisonment. "Philippians 4:13 says, 'I can do all things through Christ who strengthens me.' That meant a lot to us in Vietnam. I can assure you that whatever God asks you to do, he will provide the strength and power you need to carry on."

Paul now returns and asks prayer for Wycliffe workers around the world, stating, "Prayer is one of the most important ministries you can perform for Bible translation." He invites guests to fill out applications for membership in Wycliffe Associates which are in the program folders at every plate. Then he presents the faith promise challenge.

"You don't have to spend any money you have now. Pray

and ask God for something you don't have. Then make a promise for the amount you'd like him to supply through you during the next twelve months. This isn't a pledge; it's a faith promise. As God answers your prayer of faith, you'll receive a blessing and Wycliffe will receive help you could not otherwise have given for Bible translation.

"We don't want you to take from your church tithe. We believe the church is the base for all Christian work. We don't want you to give less to another missionary you're already supporting. Just let God lead you, and trust him to provide an extra amount for this faith promise. If he doesn't provide it, then you won't give it. It's as simple as that.

"I could tell you about a lot of people who have been blessed through making a faith promise, but I'll just mention one—a woman in California who promised ten dollars a month. The first month she was robbed on the street after cashing her paycheck. The people who gathered around saw her crying and asked why. 'I promised to give money for people without the Bible,' she explained. They gave her sixty dollars more than her paycheck. Now, we hope you won't be robbed [laughter] after making a faith promise, but we do believe you'll find it an adventure in giving.

"A faith promise card is beside your plate. Take a moment to ask God for guidance. Then put down what you believe he will provide over and above your regular income. We'll wait."

Paul sits down. The only sounds are the clinking of water glasses, occasional coughing, and the scratching of pens.

The cards are collected. Once more Paul thanks the reservation secretaries. Then he calls on a pastor to dismiss in prayer.

After the guests have left, Paul and John relax in their room. Paul talks about his family. Wife Betty works in a department store in Winston-Salem, North Carolina. Son Tony, twenty-four, is married, and daughter Paula, nineteen, is at home.

How did he become a Wycliffe Associates area director?

"I was selling women's fashions in Winston-Salem when someone invited me to a dinner like the one tonight. I heard about Wycliffe through Phil Saint, Rachel's brother, years ago, but I never felt there was anything I could do except give money and pray. God really touched my heart at that dinner. I talked to Johnny Mitchell. He invited me to help with some rallies in the area. Betty and I began to pray about full-time work. Then Johnny called me to help with dinners on the West Coast. After the first dinner, they offered me the southeast area."

He talks about the work. "It's tiring, very tiring. During the dinner meetings I'm on the road three weeks, then home one. Every night, except Sundays and Wednesdays, meeting a different audience. But the Holy Spirit keeps me going and helps me build rapport with folks I've never seen before.

"Just when I begin to get discouraged," he continues, "the Lord makes something special happen to boost my spirits.

"A young couple came late to a dinner in Daytona Beach. The only places left were at the head table, so they sat there and put their baby down. Bob Griffin of JAARS told about how a single girl translator in the Philippines had been severely injured in the crash of a government helicopter and then was healed in answer to prayer. As Bob spoke I noticed tears running down the young man's face. The next thing I knew, he and his wife were taking the Wycliffe language course. The last I heard, Wycliffe had accepted them as members in training.

"Knowing that I can have a part in involving people in Bible translation is what keeps me going."

Most faith promise dinners go off with perfect dispatch. But sometimes there are happenings which bring a dramatic touch to the occasion.

At one dinner, they had just begun eating when a Greek wedding party began in the room directly above. The chandeliers swung so violently that they feared the lights would come crashing down.

In Boston a woman walked in off the street, sat down at a vacant place, enjoyed a free dinner, and fell asleep with her head on the table. This wouldn't have been a problem, except that she snored through the entire program. Then when the benediction was pronounced, she stood up as if nothing had happened, grabbed the table decorations in front of her, and walked out.

Each of WA's other area directors (Ted Ulp, south-central; Arthur Greenleaf, northeast; Dave Houston, north-central; Stan Shaw, southwest) have humorous stories to share, most of which were not so funny at the time they occurred. But they'd rather talk about people who were enlisted for the Bible translation cause at dinners.

Some, like the young Florida couple Paul mentioned, apply for full-time or short-term service on the field. Some join work parties. Many more give money they never thought of getting.

A medical student in Dallas, being supported by his nurse wife, thought a forty-dollar-a-month faith promise would be "sufficiently out of reach without the obvious intervention of the Lord." He marked that and almost immediately forgot about it. Several days later he remembered and began to pray. His wife unexpectedly received a "merit" raise of forty-five dollars a month.

A postal employee in Memphis promised ten dollars a month which he knew he couldn't pay "without the Lord having to do something out of the ordinary." On the way home his wife mentioned that she'd promised over eight times that amount. "If the Lord doesn't give us the money, we don't owe it," she reminded him. A few weeks later he received a surprise bonus of six months' pay which had never been awarded before in the postal service.

In Oklahoma City Myron Girard, a retired electronics instructor, and his wife were living on a limited pension when they felt God leading them to make a $1,200 faith promise. A few days later Myron was repairing a dryer and found a dollar bill. "We've got only $1,199 to go," he grinned to his wife. Shortly after this he was offered a temporary job and worked long enough to pay the balance.

At the next dinner they promised another $1,200. He earned twenty dollars repairing a small diesel engine. The remaining $1,180 seemed nowhere in sight until a check for $1,800 came unexpectedly. It was from money left in a fund for Mrs. Girard years before.

They promised still another $1,200 at a third dinner. Once again Myron was given a temporary job and earned more than enough to pay the faith promise.

"When we really put God to the test," says Myron, "he always does more than we expect."

That's the faith promise spirit.

FOUR

CONSTRUCTION CREWS AND "DING-A-LINGS"

"Yarina, Yarina! We've got a teacher with a broken leg. Give me Dr. Swanson, please."

The woman in the radio tower at Wycliffe's Yarinacocha center in the Peruvian jungle flips a switch. "Roger. Hold on." She dials a phone, flips another switch, and Dr. Douglas Swanson is on the line to the Bible translator 300 miles away. "We'd better have him brought in," the doctor advises.

Grace Fuqua, the radio operator, is listening. She quickly dials the hangar, gets an OK, then radios the JAARS pilot nearest the emergency. Four hours later the Amazonian teacher is resting in the clinic. He will soon be back on the job, teaching his people the three Rs and the Scriptures in their own language.

A quarter mile from the radio tower a 200-kilowatt Waukesha generator is throbbing. Beside it a smaller reserve unit stands by in case the big generator breaks down. This is the power center, providing current for the radio tower lights, electric typewriters, printing presses, the water system, dial telephones, and home appliances. "We used to have an old belt-driven U.S. Army surplus job," old-timer Al Townsend explains. "When the engine started coughing and the lights began flickering, Les Bancroft would run out and work on it. The lights would go out and we'd have to use candles until Les got the motor going."

And before the phones? "We ran messages back and forth," says Grace Fuqua.

That was before Jack Kendall, the founder of WA's construction department, went to Peru and saw the need.

Jack was a telephone engineer and a lay preacher and prison chaplain in San Diego when recruited by Uncle Cam in December 1959. "An afternoon Wycliffe meeting was announced at church that morning," he recalls. "I wanted to take a nap after dinner, but my wife Dorothy insisted we go. After the meeting I was greeted by Uncle Cam. I'd met him briefly sometime before and he remembered my name. 'What are you doing?' he asked. 'Working for the telephone company,' I said. 'Can you come to lunch tomorrow?' I said yes without thinking.

"There Uncle Cam asked me to go to Peru and survey utility needs at the center. 'Our folks know how to translate the Bible and fly airplanes, but they need a little help with electricity, telephones, and water at the center,' he told me. I couldn't say no to him. I borrowed the money for travel and was in Peru less than two months later."

The Wycliffe workers were friendly, but didn't show much enthusiasm for a utility system. Jack looked around the center that had been carved out of the jungle, asked questions, and made notes.

They were using water from an old antiquated tank. It was gooey and green. He peeked in a few rain barrels and discovered dead frogs. "That's nothing," someone said. "We found a dead monkey in a barrel the other day. But we always boil our water before drinking it. Well, almost always."

There were no transformers on the thrown-together electrical distribution system, just wires strung along poles. The current was so weak at the end of the line that Jack almost had to strike a match to see if the light bulbs were burning.

Jack completed his survey and reported his recommendations to a Wycliffe committee as they listened skeptically.

"What you need is a complete utility system—water, electricity, and telephones," he declared. "The time you're spending now boiling water, running messages, and doing other chores that would be handled by a WET system, amounts to fourteen or fifteen people." Jack went on showing more facts and figures, hoping to build up enthusiasm. Finally he said, "I'm going home to get the equipment."

He was upset over their lack of interest. Later he learned their financial support was so low they were barely surviving, and they feared any added expense. Also, other Americans had come by, promised great things, then never returned.

Jack had some friends at the utility company in San Diego. They provided a quantity of transformers and other electrical equipment. Through other contacts, he arranged for a power company in Philadelphia to donate a big generator.

Meanwhile, a manufacturer of water purification equipment just "happened" to stop at the Peru center on a trip across South America. He examined the water system and was so appalled that he pledged to provide pumping and purification equipment.

Finally, to meet the communication need, Jack located a cast-off switchboard and dial phones in a small town in Montana.

The equipment was shipped by barge to Lima and from there trucked over the Andes. It took Jack over six years, working most of the time alone, to provide the Wycliffe center with a complete utility system.

Along the way Jack resigned his telephone company job to become a full-time construction missionary. Wycliffe gave him the title of International Technical Representative, but Jack jokingly termed himself "the Wycliffe Junk Procurer."

In 1966 Jack visited the Lomalinda center in Colombia. Here the terrain was different—with grassy mounds instead of dense jungle. But similar needs existed—a better water supply, a stepped-up, more dependable electrical system, and telephone service.

Jack was making plans for Lomalinda when Wycliffe Associates was chartered. He moved under the WA wing and took the title Director of Construction. Under his leadership, WA work crews began digging wells, stringing underground cable, and installing equipment at Lomalinda.

After the job in Colombia got started, Jack gave his attention to Wycliffe centers in Bolivia and Brazil. Wes Syverson, a veteran builder from Minnesota, went to oversee the installation of the Colombia WET system in July 1970. Three years, twenty-five miles of cable, ten miles of plastic pipe, and 5000 volunteer work hours later the job was done. Wycliffe residents at the center communicated by telephone, enjoyed steady, dependable electric power, and drank clear, sparkling water from a well, instead of murky water from a lake.

The biggest job of all came a year later in sprawling Brazil, where Wycliffe had four centers serving as jumping-off spots for translators in remote jungle villages. In just twenty-six days a highly skilled team of WA communications specialists installed telephone dial systems at the four widely separated locations. Said Jack proudly, "This is the largest mass project WA has ever attempted and is the culmination of my dream. We hope to see communications systems at all Wycliffe centers to help speed Bible translation." To this, Dorothy Kendall added, "The miracle of this doesn't register until one remembers that it took nearly seven years for Jack to install the first electrical system and dial telephone unit at the Peru center. What a difference teamwork can make!"

Associate Charles Miller, an executive with Allied Telephone Company in Little Rock, played a key role in training installers, rounding up the equipment and putting it in shape for installation, then trucking it from Little Rock to Miami for shipment to Brazil. David Reynolds, an Allied supervisor, was project foreman with assistance from Louis Stafford, a Bell Telephone troubleshooter in Little Rock. Four men from Pacific Telephone Company (Jack's old firm) came from San Diego to help. They were Don Cooper, Carl Taylor, Ed Nelson, and Glenn German. None had less than fifteen years' experience. The team was rounded out by five more Wycliffe Associates—Jim Keller, a retired Bell employee from Michigan; Bruce Sutter, a power company lineman from Iowa; Dan Chesher, a roofer from Ohio; Tony Trowbridge, WA's transportation supervisor who hauled the equipment to Miami; and Wes Syverson, the WA builder stationed in Colombia. The experienced crew laughingly called themselves "Ding-a-lings for Christ."

The men frequently worked until 3 A.M., but none complained. "This is the greatest spiritual uplift I've ever had," exulted Ed Nelson. Glenn German called Wycliffe members "the most beautiful bunch of people I've ever met." The response from indigenous believers was equally uplifting. When the crew landed at one center, a Xavante believer welcomed Glenn with open arms, calling him brother.

The importance of their work was evidenced at the Cuiaba center after they had installed an eighty-line system. The director noted, "In just thirty-five minutes I've contacted eight persons. Without the telephones, I'd have spent all day tomorrow trying to find them."

While the team moved across Brazil, Jack Kendall was home preparing equipment for a similar telephone installation in the Philippines.

News had now gotten around, and Jack was receiving requests from other missions needing help with utilities and construction. This led him to form his own organization in June 1975, the Technical Assistance Programs (TAP), under the slogan, "Tapping the resources of God through laymen." In a statement of purpose, Jack said, "TAP aims to serve evangelical missions through lay people, helping to relieve missionaries of routine or technical tasks, and giving whatever services and equipment the Lord provides to send out the gospel more quickly."

During his fifteen years with Wycliffe, Jack Kendall did much more than direct the installation of critically needed utilities at Wycliffe centers. He and his wife Dorothy held over 1500 meetings for Bible translation. They personally recruited 115 short-term assistants and volunteer workers for Wycliffe's field operations.

God had a man already prepared to take Jack's place in Wycliffe Associates, a man Jack helped recruit. Harold Leasure had long been interested in missions. A farm boy from Punxsutawney, Pennsylvania, Harold had come to California as a young teen-ager, attended barber school, passed the state examination at sixteen, and become the state's youngest licensed barber. He served with the first MASH unit in Korea, and after discharge married Juanita Ellison, a girl he met at the Church of the Open Door in Los Angeles. Then, after a stint with the Westinghouse Electric X-Ray Division in Los Angeles as field engineer, Harold obtained his own contractor's license and formed his own company, Specialty Electric.

Wycliffe was a familiar name at the Church of the Open Door. Harold and Juanita had met Uncle Cam there, along with the Nyman family and other Wycliffe personnel. But they didn't become involved with Wycliffe Associates until they moved to Orange County.

In 1972 they attended a coffee at Rey Johnson's home where Bill Butler showed films of the past year's rallies that featured Rachel Saint and the Aucas. As they were leaving, Bill said, "Harold, I'd like you to get involved with Wycliffe Associates." Harold replied, "Sure. Anytime. Let me know."

A few days later a contract to build a church fell through, and Harold was wondering what to do, when Bill asked him to "come over and look at a set of plans." The plans were for the new WA headquarters in the city of Orange, on a lot purchased from the adjoining Covenant Church.

CONSTRUCTION CREWS AND "DING-A-LINGS"

Within a week Harold was laying the foundation, and the lock and key job was completed in eighty-five days.

Harold and board chairman Rey Johnson, who personally financed the interim construction loan, were presented round-trip air tickets to Mexico City in appreciation for their commitment beyond the call of duty. The two men bought tickets for their wives and made the trip a foursome. They saw the Wycliffe headquarters, Manuel Arenas's Totonac school, and the jungle training camp. Harold had been on a mission trip once before, installing X-ray equipment for a church hospital in Hong Kong, but the construction needs of Wycliffe really challenged him.

Shortly after they got home Jack Kendall came to the Leasures' home and showed slides of his work at Wycliffe centers. "Jack opened up his heart," Harold remembers. "He wanted someone to come in and take part of the load. I told the Lord I was willing and he helped me arrange my business affairs so it could be done."

Two opportunities for service opened immediately. One was to supervise the building of additional bedrooms onto the house of Wycliffe's coordinators in Miami, Dan and Rosie Doyle. With a steady stream of Wycliffe members traveling to and from the fields, the Doyles desperately needed more room for overnight guests.

The second assignment was to take a five-man crew to Ecuador and build a house for Rachel Saint at the Limoncocha center. They landed in Quito and spent a couple of days getting ready for the jungle. Some got sick from eating new types of food, with only Harold keeping a level stomach. Then they flew across the Andes in a JAARS DC-3 and landed on the slick, grassy airstrip at Limoncocha. Stepping out of the plane, they sunk to their knees in mud.

Building Rachel's house was another new experience. The lumber was cut to size at the base sawmill just before they were ready to use it. "If you didn't nail it up quickly," Harold recalls, "it would curl up like carrot sticks. And when you hit a plank with a hammer, you had to close your eyes because it would squirt water at you. It rained twelve and a half inches while we were there, but we finished the little house, built cabinets, dug a cesspool, installed plumbing and a telephone, and did the wiring—all in five-and-a-half days. And we got another house for Rachel's partner, Rosie Jung, three-fourths done before we ran out of lumber."

Wycliffe Associates asked Harold to work under Jack Kendall as full-time coordinator of construction projects. This meant a big change for the Leasure family. With Harold on a missionary's salary, Juanita had to go to work to supplement their income. Their practice of eating out once a week at an expensive restaurant was cut to having hamburgers at McDonald's. But the joy and enrichment they shared as a family more than made up for the drop in their standard of living. Susan, twenty-one, a medical secretary and model, helped for a while as receptionist and switchboard operator at the WA office. Nancy, nineteen, worked in the WA mail room and joined a short-term medical work team to help in a clinic for the Totonac people in Mexico. And David, sixteen, accompanied his father to Guatemala to help install X-ray equipment at the Cubulco Clinic operated by nurse-translator Helen Neuenswander.

After returning from Guatemala, Harold went to Papua New Guinea to determine how WA volunteers might help speed the Word to the hundreds of linguistic groups on the mountainous island. On a trip to the interior he stopped at a denominational mission hospital and looked over their equipment. The doctor sadly pointed to a large new X-ray machine. "We've had it for three years and it's never worked."

"Perhaps I can do something," Harold said. Using only pliers and a screwdriver, he had the machine running in minutes. "It was never calibrated," he explained to the grateful missionary doctor.

Jack Kendall asked Harold to join his Technical Assistance Programs. "We can continue to help Wycliffe and other missions as well," Jack assured him. But the WA board wanted Harold to remain and take Jack's old position as director of construction and maintenance. Jack gave his blessing and Harold continued with Wycliffe Associates.

In September 1975 Harold began a monthly "Construction Bulletin" for circulation among lay people wishing to help. Needs were listed by countries.

COLOMBIA: Heavy Equipment Operators—building airstrip at Lomalinda; needed December through March.

Plumber—experienced in maintenance; able to set sinks and stools in new construction.

INDONESIA: Tools—hand tools, all types, for new base at Dahau Bira.

BOLIVIA: Dentist—work at base with Wycliffe personnel; two to six months.

BRAZIL: Masons and carpenters—work on hangar and houses at Cuiaba.

MIAMI: Carpenters/painters—help finish addition to Doyle's house in Miami; intercom system for Doyle's house.

COLOMBIA: Press Repairman—URGENT—Harris 19 x 25 offset press, model L125B, two years old, is out of adjustment (won't stay in color register). Needed in translation work.

Auto mechanic—for repair shop. All phases of maintenance and repair.

Electrician—all-around experience needed in maintenance, new installation, and motor repair.

Harold inherited a staff of three capable fieldmen. Wes Syverson, who was now given the title of superintendent of field construction, and Erv Miller, a Mennonite builder from Ohio, had been working in Colombia. John Bender, another Ohio Mennonite and building contractor, was WA's man in Brazil.

The newest challenge in Colombia was moving a large dirt mound and extending the airstrip. In one direction a pilot had to take off upgrade; then, when the plane was airborne, climb over another hill that obstructed the north end of the strip. Opting for the opposite direction, he might have to contend with a tail wind, while unable to see what was on the strip over the crest of the hill. Only the last-minute warning of an alert radio operator kept one JAARS pilot from hitting a pickup truck stalled on the far side of that hill.

JAARS had wanted the hill leveled and the strip extended since the center was built. With pilots carrying translation teams to their villages, a fatal accident would not only have meant tragic loss of life, but a setback of years in completing a New Testament. But there was never enough money available to do the job.

In 1974 a pastor and a work crew came from a church in Virginia to help build a house at the center. Their plane almost cracked up when trying to land. Before leaving, the pastor said they were going home to raise $25,000 to get the job done.

In January 1975, with help from this church and other concerned individuals, Wes Syverson and a crew of volunteers began digging away the hill with a bulldozer. The rainy season and breakdown of equipment slowed the work.

WA asked for more volunteers in the November *Newsletter*. The following January, Jay Dunteman, an experienced construction engineer from Elmhurst, Illinois, arrived with a crew. Flying around Colombia with pilot Ron Ehrenberg, Jay contracted for two dozers, a loader, grader, compactor, rippers, and three dump trucks. By the time they got the equipment to the base, Glen Shoup, a muscular young Cat operator from Mt. Eaton, Ohio, had arrived with another crew, vowing to stay until the hill was removed and the extended strip graded and ready for traffic.

CONSTRUCTION CREWS AND "DING-A-LINGS"

Wes and Glen worked full time while crews came and went as their stateside vacation times permitted. With shifts going day and night, the hill shrank faster, but equipment breakdowns kept delaying the work, and when time to leave drew near for the last crew, it looked as if completion might be held up for many more precious months.

A plea went out for more help, and men from Emmanuel Faith Community Church in Escondido, California, responded. (The church's pastor, Rev. Richard Strauss, had recently been to Colombia as the branch's conference speaker.) The church agreed to help pay expenses, and wives and children gave their support so the men could go. One family even used $800 set aside for their vacation. By March 1976 the hill was gone; an estimated 75,000 yards of hard, sticky clay had been moved! As soon as the gravel surface was put on, planes could begin using the extended strip.

With the dump trucks parked and the big dozer motors silent, the last crew stood looking at what they had done. Reflecting later, Royce Wale seemed to express everyone's feelings: "As I stood there on our last day, looking toward the horizon, I thought about the tribes beyond those hills and realized the center was here because of them. We were really thankful to have had a small part in seeing the job finished and making it safer for the flights in and out of Lomalinda."

Only one serious accident marred the work. A young Ohioan drowned while swimming in the lake. But in God's plan, a Christian mortician was at the center to care for the body and arrange for transport back to Ohio for burial. The mortician had come only the day before to drive a dump truck, never knowing that his professional services would be needed so soon.

Meanwhile, WA's two other full-time construction men were busy in Brazil. Erv Miller had first worked in Colombia as a member of a work party. There he fell in love with a girl visiting her translator sister. They returned to the U.S., got married, and went to Brazil.

WA's third fieldman, John Bender, had been challenged

by Bill Butler and Jack Kendall. John and his wife Liz sold their construction business, moved to Brazil, and built a house at the Porto Velho Center. John has since helped many Wycliffe members build their own houses and has superintended work crews at several Brazil centers. When a back ailment made it impossible to continue the strenuous field work, John and his family moved to Southern California and John became field director for construction.

Harold and John can call on hundreds of volunteers to assist Wycliffe members on the fields. Mennonite groups from northern Ohio and Big Valley, Pennsylvania, have made numerous trips to South America. Baptist and Methodist farmers, as well as tradesmen from around downstate Illinois, have contributed much sweat and muscle. Associates from Sarasota, Florida, helped in Miami and Ecuador. WA teams from Arizona, Iowa, and California drove a caravan of work vehicles to Guatemala and helped translators rebuild village homes damaged or destroyed during the 1976 catastrophic earthquake. And from North Carolina a team of surveyors and engineers, led by Merlyn ("Megs") Giddings, surveyed lands for the Indian tribes in Colombia, Ecuador, and Brazil.

Many more have contributed equipment from a value of a few dollars to surplus material that would cost hundreds of thousands if it had to be purchased new. Some company owners have assigned their men to WA construction jobs, paying their travel expenses and wages.

The repository of interesting stories from WA construction people would fill volumes. We can only relate a few in this chapter.

There is the incident that Megs Giddings and his land surveying crew laugh about now, but which was not so funny at the time. They were surveying land for the Cuiba people deep in the Colombian jungle. Tired from dragging their heavy chain and other equipment through the thick underbrush, they lay down in the hot afternoon to rest. Suddenly they heard the whir of wings and looked up to see a flock of ravenous vultures descending. "They think we're dead!" Megs shouted. "Let's get out of here!"

CONSTRUCTION CREWS AND "DING-A-LINGS"

Travel stories abound. The famous seventy-five mile Andean taxi ride from Bogota, Colombia, to Villavicencio (for pickup by a JAARS plane for the flight to Lomalinda) is unforgettable. Hurtling along the narrow strip of pavement carved along high canyon walls, more than one Associate has experienced heavy stomach turbulence.

But nothing tops the experience of a Brazil-bound Ohio construction crew of eight Mennonites and two Amish men recruited by John Hostetler, a Wycliffe community development worker in Brazil.

They first planned to drive to Miami and pick up a commercial flight to South America. But at the last minute they learned of a Smithsonian Institution DC-3 plane available for hire to nonprofit groups. The plane had one new engine and the other had been completely reconditioned.

A freezing rain was falling when they arrived at the Akron-Canton Airport about 5:30 A.M., February 2, 1974, for the nonstop flight to Florida. Smithsonian pilot "Rocky" LeRogue took off at 6:10. Minutes later, at 5000 feet, he saw that the oil pressure on the left engine had dropped to zero. When the engine temperature reached the danger point he shut the engine off and radioed back to the airport for emergency landing instructions. But the runways were now glazed with ice and the flight controller instructed him to head for Pittsburgh, eighty miles away.

Suddenly the other engine began sputtering and backfiring. Passengers on the right side saw bursts of flame. It was overheated and could explode at any minute, bringing disaster. Now, running only on the weakened engine, the plane was losing altitude fast.

Some of the passengers did not realize the danger. But the pilot's wife, sitting in the front of the plane, did. Quickly wrapping herself in a blanket, she turned to John Hostetler and said tensely, "This is really serious. Can't you sing or pray, or do something?"

Hostetler turned to face the others. "Boys, we're in serious trouble. Let's pray." They prayed, then they began singing, "My Faith Looks Up to Thee," as the plane sank lower and lower.

The pilot was on the radio asking for the location of the nearest airfield. There seemed only one chance—try to start the left, overheated engine. Rocky explained that it was "probably froze up and if it isn't, we're liable to have fire. Keep praying." He pressed the starter and the engine came to life.

With one eye on the temperature of the left engine (because it was running without oil), he dropped toward a small airstrip and touched down gently. When he turned off the engines there were no cheers, just a deathly quiet as everyone thanked God for his protection. The pilot looked around and remarked solemnly, "That left engine should never have started. And as hot as the other engine was, it could have exploded in midair. God must have been on our side."

Ten minutes later the runway was glazed with ice. They had landed just in time.

They went home and regrouped, with most deciding to continue to Miami by car. The Arab oil embargo was on and gas was critically scarce. Instead of traveling the interstate highways, they kept to back roads where they thought gas might be more available. They saw more closed than open stations and at times wondered if they would ever reach Florida. Once, when one of the two cars was running on empty, they pulled into a station as the owner was closing up. "Aw, what the heck," he said after hearing their story. "I can squeeze one more tankful out."

Sunday morning they stopped at a small Baptist church and had the opportunity to tell about their trip. The pianist was amazed. "I've never heard of Wycliffe Bible Translators," she said. "I didn't know there was anyone left in the world without the Bible." Then she gave them a check for their gasoline expenses.

Arriving in Miami, they got seats on an old World War II "Flying Turtle" prop plane. It took them to Belem, on the northeast coast of Brazil. There they boarded a Brazilian Air Force plane for the Apalai location where they were to build a house for translators Ed and Sally Koehn. They walked right into a hepatitis epidemic, but managed to get the house built. Then Glen Shoup and two others decided to return to Belem to build some private Wycliffe housing.

A Brazilian Air Force plane flew them part way, dropping them off at a remote airstrip where a crowd of people had been waiting several days for a plane. They were instructed to put their names at the bottom of the list. It appeared that they might be stranded for six weeks or longer.

A Mission Aviation Fellowship plane landed. "I can't take you to Belem," the pilot said. "Just keep praying and I'll see if I can get you some help." He flew away, leaving the lonely threesome wondering if they would ever get out of the jungles.

A couple of days later they heard the roar of motors. A gleaming, freshly painted DC-3 landed. It was obviously no ordinary plane. There was a gold insignia on the side, and when the door opened a squad of soldiers stepped out smartly and marched over to where the WA crew, still wearing dirty jeans and T-shirts, were sitting. The associates didn't understand Portuguese, but they realized that the soldiers wanted them to get on the plane.

The soldiers escorted them across the field and ushered them inside the luxurious cabin. Seated all around were officers wearing stars and gold braid.

A short while later the plane landed at Belem where a couple of Wycliffe members were waiting. "This just doesn't happen to missionaries," one said to Glen in amazement. "You were flying on the general's plane. He's in charge of this whole territory."

Glen and his two friends were equally astonished. "We didn't know," Glen replied. "We don't speak Portuguese. Maybe we should go thank him."

They walked back to the plane where the general was standing with several other officers and thanked him in English. The general grinned and then winked as if he had pulled off a practical joke. But it was no joke to the Ohioans. They could only say, "Praise the Lord! God takes care of his own."

FIVE

DOWN ON THE FARM

Lay assistance to Wycliffe's farm program goes back to the early 1930s when Will Townsend mailed packets of seed for his son's "demonstration" garden in Mexico.

When Cam started work among the Aztecs in Tetelcingo, he planted a model garden in the village square. He had the Aztecs bring manure, bat dung, and ashes to the plaza to replenish the thin soil. Then he asked the mayor to hold a town meeting to see what the citizens needed. Cam wrote everything down and went to Mexico City and got vegetable seeds and young fruit trees from friends in the government.

With the Aztecs watching, Cam planted, fertilized, irrigated, and weeded until the once-barren ground became a horticulturist's paradise of lettuce, radishes, celery, beets, and fruit. Seeing was believing and it wasn't long before the villagers were making their own gardens and enhancing their diet beyond tortillas, chilies, and beans. Cam had set off a veritable agricultural revolution in the village.

President Lazaro Cardenas heard about it and came to see. As they walked through the garden, Cam talked about his hope of bringing American youth to Mexico to translate the Bible into Indian languages. "Will they help the Indians in the practical way you are doing?" the President asked. When Cam said they would, Cardenas urged, "Bring all you can get."

At a critical time in Mexican-U.S. relations, when regular missionaries were being turned back at the border, Cam's young friends were welcomed with warm *abrazos* (embraces) by Mexican officialdom.

When Cam led a new group of Bible translators to Peru, he naturally planted vegetables and set out fruit trees around his house. By this time Wycliffe had grown so large that the general director could not spend the time he wished with the soil. Instead he reminded Wycliffe members of how his "cabbage patch" had opened doors in Mexico and urged them to establish a farm at the center.

The members were slow catching on. Bible translation to them was so urgent that they couldn't see the importance of "Uncle Cam's cabbage patch," as everyone called the idea. When nobody acted, Cam recruited a young agriculturist, Herb Fuqua, from California. Herb arrived and still nobody got excited. "It's like I have a saddle, but no horse," he complained to Uncle Cam.

"Go ahead," Cam pressed. "I'll give you all the help I can."

Cam's travels took him to Chicago where he called on friends and spoke to students at the Moody Bible Institute. A young student from downstate Illinois introduced herself to Cam. He asked about her family. When she mentioned that her brother was going to visit the big LeTourneau farm project in Peru, Cam's eyes snapped with interest. "Maybe he could take something down to our folks. He'll be going right near our center."

The brother was Dean Puzey from the little farming community of Fairmount near the Indiana border. Cam talked with him a few minutes about jungle farming, then handed him a package. "Please take good care of it. And look up Herb Fuqua, our agriculturist. You and he should have a lot in common."

Dean delivered the package—three boxes of prunes. Then he met Herb, who showed him around and explained how agriculture was connected to Bible translation. "We started with translators. Then we had to have planes to move them around. But what good is a New Testament without readers? So we got into schools and adult literacy. Follow?"

Dean nodded. "Always before the people had been nomads, hunting for game, clearing land and planting a crop or two, then moving on. But when schools were started, they began establishing permanent villages which created health and food problems.

"Living in villages means they have less hunting territory. The game supply is soon exhausted. And they have less land to farm, since they don't know how to rotate crops or fertilize."

Herb presented his dreams. "We want to teach them modern farming methods and help them get more out of the soil than they're getting. Also bring in some calves and pigs which they can buy out of a revolving loan fund.

"Uncle Cam," Herb continued, "would like to see a demonstration and training farm in every South American country where we have a Wycliffe branch. We have land and some livestock and crops here, as you can see. Our other branches aren't that far along."

The Illinois farmer was eager to help. "I'm going home to talk to my brothers," he assured. "Maybe there's something we can do."

Dean Puzey's initial trip to South America marked the beginning of a long involvement by the four Puzey brothers and other farmers around Fairmount, Illinois. None ever became Wycliffe members, but in the two decades since Dean's visit to the Peru center, they have bought and leased land and sent machinery and animals worth tens of thousands of dollars.

The four brothers—Marvin, Lloyd, Lowell, and Dean—were from a family that had farmed the rich black Illinois land for four generations. They raised principally corn with an average yield of over 150 bushels per acre. Now they entered into an unusual partnership and opened a machine shop to manufacture farm machinery. Profits, they agreed, would be divided five equal ways between themselves and the Lord.

Some of God's share from the first profits went to purchase a John Deere tractor for the new Wycliffe center under construction in Ecuador. The tractor was shipped by ocean freight to a port, then dismantled and flown over the Andes to the jungle center in crates. About the same time the Mossy Rock Community Church in Washington State gave the Limoncocha center a small sawmill. With the Puzey brothers' tractor providing the power, the mill produced the lumber for the first houses at the center.

The brothers didn't believe in keeping a good thing to themselves. They told their customers and neighbors. Soon farmers from fifty miles around were contributing money and equipment to Wycliffe farm programs in South America. Men in Dean's Baptist church became involved and went on work trips. In Big Valley, Pennsylvania, a group of hard-working Mennonite farmers became interested. Between these Mennonites and the Fairmount farmers a sort of partnership evolved. The Pennsylvanians would provide the livestock and the Illinoisans the farm equipment.

Lowell Puzey took along his Catholic dentist on one work trip to Lomalinda, Colombia. In three days, Dr. Stephen Chantos put in 300 fillings.

The coalition of farmers, under Lowell's leadership, sort of adopted the Lomalinda center for their own farm project. In 1966 Lowell and three friends purchased for $12,000 about a thousand acres of farmland across a swamp from Lomalinda. They named the farm Bonaire, after the Christian radio station to which the previous owner faithfully listened.

They leased the land to Wycliffe for a nominal charge. Farm operation was assigned to an agricultural committee of WBT members, with Lowell and his friends serving only as advisers.

There was plenty of work to do. Old fence lines had

decayed or disappeared. The banana patch was a thicket and needed cleaning. An irrigation system was required for the rice crop during the summer and winter dry seasons. A new farmhouse and an office were needed with power lines stretched across the swamp from the base power supply. A barn was needed for animals. Dining, classroom, and dorm facilities for indigenous students, and equipment for farm operation were essential.

After almost three years of planning, praying, and working, the old farm was transformed into the most outstanding indigenous training facility in South America. The smelly chicken house was modernized and enlarged into a new office building. The stable was transformed into a dining-classroom complex. The old feed room became the first classroom. New staff housing was constructed. All the while, farming and livestock raising continued.

Volunteer labor by WA work crews from the United States cut construction costs to a fraction of what the buildings would otherwise have cost. Most of the volunteers came from around Fairmount, Illinois, and Big Valley, Pennsylvania, but some came from California and other states.

Greg Henderson, a twenty-one-year-old Cal Poly student from Santa Ana, California, spent a summer helping build the office facility. Greg reported back to Wycliffe Associates: "I worked entirely with a Colombian who didn't know English, so I learned some Spanish." Greg also learned to butcher hogs Colombian style. "They have no way to cool meat, so within a few hours of slaughtering we had to deliver it to the homes at the center." Another new experience was learning to milk cows by hand, then delivering the milk by motorcycle over a bumpy road.

He mentioned the cattle, goats, and pigs, gifts from Mennonite churches in Pennsylvania and Heifer Projects. And the training program getting under way where some forty villagers were learning how to build fences, what to feed animals, and how to treat livestock diseases. "One

Colombian official," Greg said, "got so excited that he promised to supply barbed wire and fifty head of cattle if the villagers would learn how to care for the livestock."

Greg was so enthusiastic that he traveled 2400 miles by motorcycle across the United States telling about the farm program at Lomalinda.

Herb Brussow, a lean, energetic Californian, and his wife Mickey, came from Bolivia to direct the Colombia farm operations. Lowell Puzey flew down for a conference.

"I know how important agriculture is to jungle people," Herb told Lowell. "I remember the first time I saw a baby dying of malnutrition. The stomach was protruding, the arms and legs were like matchsticks, and it was barely alive. When I came back the next day the baby was dead. A better diet could have saved that child's life."

Herb and Lowell suggested that the farm at Lomalinda be a training center. "Translators can bring in ambitious men from the villages," Lowell said. "Then after they complete their courses, send them back as extension agents to their people."

Herb said he "couldn't agree more. I say it's better to teach a man to farm than to give him the food. If you give him commodities he becomes a sponge and looks to the next handout. But if you teach him to farm, he can live today, tomorrow, and next year."

In the mid-seventies, under Herb's direction, Bonaire became a mecca of hope for teaching Amazonians with dwindling food supplies to become self-sufficient. About fifty students from fifteen to twenty villages are now being trained in each six-week session. The students rise at 6 A.M. for breakfast and then go off to class. They study poultry, cattle, and swine raising and learn how to improve production of crops. One "must" for completing the course is learning how to develop a compost pile.

The students are not left to fend for themselves in their villages. They consult with their resident Bible translators and talk to Herb and other farm staff by radio. Herb and other staff members make periodic fly-in visits much like county agents do in the U.S.

Gifts from friends in the United States have made available gift animals to villagers who complete courses in livestock raising. A Kwaiker man expressed his appreciation for a gift pig in his own style of free verse as literally translated:

Here at this place thus he gave to me.
One pig, that is, one sow, one boar he gave to me.

This is a good breed, they say, It's a pretty breed.
This is not from here, they say.
It is brought from afar.
For breeding it was sent that we might have
      that they all among us might breed their own.
And now we also have heard them say to us the
      same thing: that among all the Indians they
      might benefit by breeding that we might have
      large pigs.

Giving it free he gave.
And there (in the tribe) they are not willing to give
      like this.
Here they gave.

Those at the farm are helping the owners of the
      pigs who live far away.
They are not here.

And now I shall say like this.

      Like him (who sent the pigs), I have.
      If I want to sell, I could sell.
      First raising, if I want to eat, I could eat.
      How might it be? Will they be raised?

Now to those who give (pigs), I am sending word
      (my mouth)
To all those for giving these, thanks—good he
      gave.
To all those I am advising for giving these.

Thanks, I say.
It's done.

The success of the Bonaire farm has brought visitors from throughout Colombia and other countries. Mickey Brussow serves refreshments to about a hundred guests a month. Many are Colombian officials who take back glowing reports to their superiors in Bogota, the Colombian capital.

Indeed, Herb Brussow has become more of a celebrity than he likes. Political agitators have labeled him a major in the American CIA and accused him of killing Che Guevara. The absurd stories being spread point to the farm's importance.

As in other Latin American countries, Wycliffe works under contract with the national Ministry of Education. Lowell Puzey and other friends in the U.S. recognize this and do not speak of Bonaire as their farm. As Lowell puts it, "We only want to lend a helping hand."

Lending a helping hand to Wycliffe has become a big operation for the Puzeys. Back in Fairmount they have a warehouse full of equipment, some donated by themselves and some by other farmers and implement dealers. Here the equipment is inspected, cleaned, adjusted and, if necessary, repaired for shipment to Miami where it will go by barge or ship to South America.

Lowell and Dean make periodic trips to the fields. Lowell has been to the Bonaire farm in Colombia at least twenty-five times and has visited farms in other countries as well.

They have brought back numerous artifacts. Their best office conversation pieces are the skin of a huge boa stretched across a wall and a stuffed tarantula larger than a man's hand that rests on a desk.

They carry items back and forth for Wycliffe members, much as Dean took the package of prunes to Peru on his first trip. "We don't carry contraband," Lowell stresses. "Mostly it's stuff that would take too long or might be lost going through regular channels." By far the most precious item Lowell ever handled was the original manuscript of the Auca New Testament which he brought to the U.S. for printing.

Lowell and Dean regularly have Wycliffe guests in their homes. During the summer of 1976 Lowell's family had forty-five such visitors.

Among the scores of friends the Puzeys have enlisted in the aid program to Wycliffe farm operations, none has meant more to Wycliffe than Joe Ashbrook.

Lowell first took Joe, a longtime friend, to the JAARS center in North Carolina and introduced him to Uncle Cam. After hearing Cam describe what Wycliffe was doing, Joe wrote a $500 check and started to hand it to the Wycliffe founder. "You can't get off that easy," Lowell exclaimed with a grin, as he took the check and tore it up. "You're good for a lot more."

After a trip to Colombia, Joe was really hooked. "Does Wycliffe have centers in Brazil?" he asked. Lowell assured him there were four.

"Well, I'd like to take one of them and do there what you fellows have done in Colombia."

Joe's interest in South America goes back almost forty years. After graduating from the University of Illinois in 1932, he managed meat packing plants in Ecuador, Argentina, and Brazil. In Brazil he became acquainted with a U.S. consular agent who persuaded him to become coordinator for the U.S. Point Four Aid program in Brazil. One of his projects was to help the Brazilian Government feed rubber workers in northeast Brazil.

After two years with Uncle Sam, he returned to Illinois and started a corn cob processing business. By 1970 he had ten plants and was looking toward retirement.

The Wycliffe program appealed to Joe for two reasons. One, he liked the people-to-people approach which, as he told the Puzeys, "is more effective than government aid because it reaches the poor people where they are." Two, he admired Wycliffe's way of relating Christianity to physical and social needs. "I never thought before that missionaries were trying to improve the basic living conditions of the people."

Joe selected the Wycliffe center at Porto Velho, which is located on a tributary of the Amazon, far back in the bush. The area was so thinly settled that it was still a territory and under the supervision of the Brazilian military.

He bought 740 acres for a farm and sold a little over half to the Brazilian Air Force. Then he leased additional acreage from the Air Force which adjoined the other side of the farm. With the help of Mennonite volunteers from Pennsylvania, the land was fenced and a cattle herd started. The Brazilian brigadier general in command over the area was so impressed that he gave the center three water buffalo.

"We're a few years behind Colombia," Joe concedes, "but we're catching up fast. We intend to train Brazilian tribesmen as is done at Bonaire. They'll take seed and livestock back with them to their villages and show their people how to improve their economy."

Joe realizes, as do the Puzey brothers, that other help is needed. He has enlisted assistance from the agriculture department at the University of Illinois and also hopes to get Purdue University in Indiana and other agencies working on the Brazil project.

Firsthand involvement with missions has revitalized Joe's spiritual life. "I was sort of a minus Presbyterian before this came along. It has drawn me to a closer walk with the Lord. I've found that loving the Lord means helping other people, really helping them. And this gives a satisfaction which encourages me to go further."

Joe has also found that "you can't outgive God. About a month ago I went to clip some school bond coupons and found one group of bonds had matured. This gave us the capital for some improvements at Porto Velho. Yesterday I needed more capital. I checked some old railroad stock and found that it has more than doubled in worth in the past thirty days. I'm selling the stock so we'll have money to go ahead with our project. It seems that just when we need more finances, out of a clear blue sky the money turns up."

Joe sees himself and other lay workers as "partners with the missionaries who are busy preparing the written Word for the tribespeople. We can do things they can't. And in our involvement we are introducing the Living Word. There are enough Christians in the U.S. to change the world, if we could just get them involved."

One who is personally involved in Ecuador is Dr. John Bishop. John holds a Ph.D. in tropical veterinary medicine from Texas A & M and has worked for the Ford and Rockefeller Foundations and the U.S. Agency for International Development. A Lutheran layman, he went to Ecuador in 1972 from the University of Florida as a technical adviser to the Ecuadorian government. His mission was to set up a research and training program in livestock production in the lowland tropics.

He met Wycliffe's John Lindskoog, director of the Ecuador branch, at the English Fellowship Church in Quito. Lindskoog suggested he "see what we're doing with the Ministry of Education at Limoncocha."

Dr. Bishop took his family to the center where they met Joe Blakeslee, the Wycliffe agriculturist. Since Joe's specialty was plants and John's was animals, it seemed they could have an ideal partnership in setting up a demonstration farm. Furthermore, the Bishops could send their children to school with the Wycliffe kids at the center. They could share in the group Bible study and worship with the Wycliffe members and help out wherever they were needed.

The University of Florida, through the Ecuadorian government, would pay John half salary on which he could support himself. He would then be free to give half of his time to Wycliffe. The National Science Foundation in the U.S. would provide a grant for expenses in developing the model farm.

The model farm is now being developed on fifty hectares (about 150 acres), which is the current Ecuadorian homestead size set by the government's Land Reform Law. It includes crop, livestock, and forest production and involves five subsystems, from one-half to forty hectares in size.

The Quechua-style house John recently completed for his family from materials available in the jungle sits on a half hectare of land. Surrounding the house are grapefruit, lemon, tangerine, orange, avocado, and other native fruit trees which will bear fruit from one to two years after planting. Another half hectare unit is planted in peanuts which will be rotated every year with grass and vines for livestock food and fencing. A third unit of one hectare size will support multiple cropping (perennials) of plantain, banana, papaya, taro, and sweet potatoes in rotation with feed crops. A fourth unit of eight hectares is set aside for corn, cowpea, and squash in rotation with feed crops and for grazing by hogs, ducks, and cattle. The largest unit of forty hectares is reserved for raising native trees (laurel, cedar, bamboo, cashew, etc.) for shade, fruit, fiber, nuts, and construction materials. John estimates that from eight to sixteen years will be required to establish the native trees.

As the farm advances, John and his colleague plan to bring Ecuadorian farmers in for training. "We hope they will go home, develop their own farms, and convince others," John says. "If this is successful in the vast tropical lowlands, gigantic steps could be taken in solving the food problems of the central Andean countries of Ecuador, Peru, and Bolivia."

"If we can go to the moon, we can learn to farm in the Amazon," he continues, adding: "This is one mission in which Christians should have a part."

The Puzey brothers, Joe Ashbrook, John Bishop, and other Wycliffe farm supporters agree.

MISSIONS OF MERCY

Wycliffe Associates had hardly been born when a disturbing letter came from translators Ken and Elaine Jacobs in southern Mexico.

"Over forty Chamulas have been driven from their homes. They're sleeping in every available space in our one-bedroom house. One family is in the corn bin; another in the wheat bin. We're running out of food...."

The Jacobses explained that the Chamula area was a stronghold of paganism. The elders had once impaled a witch doctor's young son on a cross and proclaimed him as their savior. No Christian missionaries, or any other outsiders had ever been permitted to live within their borders. But a young man, Domingo, had come to the Jacobses' house seeking work and had stayed two years to help them translate the Gospel of Mark into the Chamula dialect. When he went back to share his new faith, a witch doctor threatened him with death. Severe persecution followed until Domingo's family and other believers had to flee for their lives.

"When they came to us," the Jacobses wrote, "They had nowhere to go and nothing to eat. We had to take them in."

From gifts designated "where needed most," Wycliffe Associates sent $300 immediately. An appeal was made and other help followed.

Mexican officials ordered the Chamula elders to let the exiles return, "or we will send in soldiers."

The elders grudgingly backed down, but said they could not guarantee the safety of the Christians at night. The believers went back. One night a band of vengeful Chamula men crept to the home of a Christian family and set the thatch roof afire. The parents had left four young children in the care of an eighteen-year-old girl. Two children were killed and the young woman and two others seriously wounded.

The young woman recovered and later came to the U.S. with one of the surviving children to thank Wycliffe Associates for the help given.*

The love offering for the suffering Chamulas was WA's first emergency mission of mercy. The second was more personal and complex.

Little Elena Arroyo, the ninth of eleven children of Otomi parents in central Mexico, was born without ears. Only a tiny bit of lobe on one side of her head indicated where that ear should be. The other side of her head was smooth.

It was the custom in the village to allow a deformed baby to die. Such a baby indicated that the parents had done something wrong—perhaps the child was illegitimate.

"Don't cut the cord and she will bleed to death," one neighbor advised. Another said, "Just don't feed her and she'll die."

Fortunately the parents were Christians. "The Lord has a purpose in giving this little one to us," the father said. "If she can't do anything else, she can sit at the door and keep the chickens out of the house."

Translator Vola Griste, who lived in the house next door, was away. When she returned to the village she tenderly examined the baby, then handed her back to her mother. "When she's old enough," Vola promised, "I'll take her out to a doctor and see what can be done."

Little Elena learned to walk normally and to communi-

*For the up-to-date story of the new Chamula church, read *They Dared to Be Different*, by Hugh Steven (Harvest House, $2.95).

cate with Vola by hand gestures. But she could hear only vibrations. The catcalls of other children, who named her "the crippled one," never bothered her.

When she was five, Vola and her parents took her down the steep mountain trail to the market town. There the parents signed papers releasing her to Vola's guardianship. The next day Vola and Elena boarded a small single-engine bush plane for the flight to Mexico City.

Vola took Elena to the local Shriner's Hospital where doctors looked at the little girl sadly. "We aren't trained and equipped to do the surgery she must have," they said. "You'll have to take her to the States."

At the Wycliffe headquarters they were going through the serving line in the dining hall when a smiling woman behind the counter noticed Elena and asked about her problem. When Vola told her, the woman exclaimed, "Oh, I have a doctor friend back in Oklahoma City. I'll write him right away." Caroline Buntz explained that while her husband Len was working in Mexico City for a few months, she was serving as a guest helper. Both had been active in the Wycliffe Associates chapter in Oklahoma City.

Vola and Elena remained in Mexico City. About a week later Caroline came running to their room. "He said bring Elena to Oklahoma City and he'll see what he can do."

Vola now had to get permission to take Elena out of the country. This meant returning to the village for signed authorization by the village mayor and Elena's parents; then going back to Mexico City where they had to wait several more weeks for traveling papers. Finally they were on their way.

Dr. David Stewart and his associate Dr. Jack Hough immediately fell in love with Elena. But before she could be operated on, they said, she would have to be X-rayed by a special machine available only in Chicago and one other city. It seemed providential that Vola was already scheduled to participate in a missionary conference in Chicago.

She and Elena drove to Chicago where the X-rays were made without charge. Then after the missionary conference at Mayfair Bible Church, they returned to Oklahoma City.

The delicate surgery at Presbyterian Hospital involved opening a channel to her inner ear, making an eardrum with skin transplanted from her leg, and connecting tiny bones that had never been fused together properly. The doctors weren't very confident. "We'll just have to wait," Dr. Hough said.

Elena was returned to her room in the pediatrics section. Vola slept on a cot beside her bed as she had prior to the surgery. That night a child crying across the hall woke Vola up. She heard sounds coming from Elena's bed. Could it be coincidence, or had the crying also awakened Elena?

By this time the little girl without ears had become a subject of widespread interest in Oklahoma City. One of the many gifts she received was a toy cash register. One day Dr. Stewart walked by the room and heard repeated "ding-a-lings." He looked inside and there was Elena sitting up in bed punching buttons and grinning at each ring. "That thrilled me more than any sound I had ever heard in my life," he later told friends. "I knew she was hearing."

Her hearing kept improving. She laughed at sounds she enjoyed, especially the mention of her name. An Oklahoma City newspaper headlined a feature story, "Lend an Ear to a Miracle."

The doctors had donated their services, but the hospital bill had to be paid. An appeal ran in the Wycliffe Associates *Newsletter* and money began coming in. Associate Floyd Wroughton sent several checks from Springfield, Illinois, explaining they were from money placed in Sunday school "mite boxes" for Elena. The hospital bill was paid.

When the bandages were taken off, Vola took Elena back to Mexico to allow time for healing. News of Elena's successful operation traveled ahead of them. Her picture was in a Mexico City newspaper along with an account of the surgery.

While they waited in Mexico, an appeal went out from WA for plastic ears. A California company responded. Now Vola took Elena to California where she was fitted with her new flesh-colored ears.

Back in her village her older brother Augustano preached a sermon to the Otomi believers about the man born blind whose sight Jesus restored. "Jesus said it was so the works of God could be made manifest in him," Augustano declared. "It is the same with Elena. She was born without ears so the glory of the Lord could be made known."

Elena, listening, smiled her assent.

Jim Olson, a member of a WA work party at the Limoncocha center in Ecuador, discovered the plight of Emma, a young Cofan woman. Jim, an Evangelical Free Church layman, was introduced to Emma by translator Bub Borman. "She's our first Cofan missionary to her people," Borman glowed. "She uses flannelgraphs of Paul's journeys with our Cofan translation of Acts. And she also helps us check translation.

"The Cofans have been very difficult to reach," Bub went on. "Before we came in 1955 the last outsider who tried to live among them was a Catholic priest in about 1600. He was killed. Now with young people like Emma coming up, we believe they are going to be responsive to the gospel."

As Emma limped away, Jim asked curiously, "Why does she wear those long red leggings in this jungle heat?"

"She has an artificial leg," Borman replied. "Started with a snake bite."

Jim wanted to hear the whole story.

"Emma lives in a village way upriver," Bub explained. "The snake, a fer-de-lance, hit her one night in the dark. They put a tourniquet on her leg, blew smoke, and did all the other witch doctor stuff, but she got no better. The fer-de-lance causes internal bleeding, and she was bleeding from her pores, eyes, nose, everywhere. Her father became desperate and took her to the military post at Santa Cecilia. He got there just as our plane landed to deliver a message. It was God's planning. Couldn't have been timed better.

"Our pilot brought her here and several of us gave blood for transfusions in the clinic. Lois Pederson, our nurse, could see that her foot was numb and black and probably gangrenous. So she sent her on out to the HCJB mission hospital at Shell Mera. To save her life they amputated five inches below her knee.

"Folks at Shell witnessed to her about the Lord. When she came back to our house to recuperate, my wife Bobbie and I had more opportunities to tell her about Jesus. Bobbie taught her to read and then we took her to Quito and had her fitted with an artificial limb. But that didn't prove too satisfactory."

"What was the problem?" Jim asked.

"The humidity, for one thing. It kept rotting away. And her leg kept growing. I lengthened the artificial extension six times, gluing wood between the two sections and fiberglassing over the top. She needs a new leg . . . badly."

"Maybe Wycliffe Associates can help," Jim encouraged.

Back in the U.S. Jim started the wheels rolling. The WA *Newsletter* asked for $2,000, plus medical expenses, for round-trip transportation for Emma and Bobbie Borman to Miami. Jim, Harold Leasure, and another work party member, Wally Johnson, gave talks at churches in Southern California. And Dan Doyle, Wycliffe's coordinator in Miami, arranged for hospitality with Mary Wadsworth, Louie Ebersole, and other associates in nearby Sarasota.

A new leg was fitted, and today Emma is one of two bilingual schoolteachers among the Cofan people.

A similar mission of mercy was sparked by a letter to WA business manager Doug Meland. It was from a Brazilian Indian agent who lived among the Fulnio people in the town of Aguas Belas, Pernambuco, where Doug and his wife Doris had worked before returning to the States. The agent had helped the Melands on many occasions, providing them a house and helping them get acquainted with the Fulnio people. Now he was asking a favor.

"My son, you remember, was in medical school. He graduated and was practicing medicine when he lost his arm in an automobile accident. Could you help him get an artificial arm?"

Doug talked to others at the Wycliffe Associates office. They decided that helping the young Brazilian, Dr. Sebastian Mendonça, was a worthy project. Out went an appeal in the Newsletter for funds to pay medical expenses.

Doug knew that the Brazilian airline Varig had helped in similar situations. He called the president of the company that represented the airline in New York City and explained the need. "Write me a letter and I'll see what I can do," he said. The airline provided a ticket covering both the domestic and international flight.

When young Dr. Mendonça arrived in Los Angeles, doctors examined him free and arranged for a hospital to provide the prosthesis. Wycliffe Associates had to pay only for the artificial arm and some miscellaneous travel expense. In four weeks the Brazilian medic was back home practicing medicine with two arms.

Through the early seventies requests kept coming to Wycliffe Associates to aid in other mercy missions.

Most came from Wycliffe workers on the field. For example, translator Herman Aschmann inquired from Totonac country in Mexico "if Wycliffe Associates can find a doctor in the States to help Pastor Miguel Cano's eye problem." Herman recalled that WA had previously contributed $200 to add a kitchen to the pastor's tumbledown house. Now cataracts were forming on his eyes. Wycliffe Associates found someone and surgery was arranged.

The first Totonac believer, Manuel Arenas, was known to thousands of Wycliffe Associates who had read his biography by Hugh Steven or heard him speak at faith promise dinners. The Totonac Bible Center he founded had benefited from gifts from many associates. In late 1975 this dynamic spiritual leader of his people began suffering from constant back pains. He got to where he could not sit at all and could stand only for short periods before having to lie flat on his back.

Mexican doctors recommended surgery in the United States, and Manuel flew to California where he had friends among Wycliffe Associates. Harold Leasure, a member of the Totonac Bible Center board, arranged for examinations with Dr. Wendell Searer at Buenaventura Medical Clinic. Dr. Searer and his colleagues concluded that a congenital problem in Manuel's spine had caused two discs to rupture. He should have immediate surgery.

Far from home and in a foreign country, Manuel fretted about where the money would come from for the expensive surgery and long hospitalization required. He felt it would be too much for Wycliffe Associates. They had so many other calls to answer.

"Don't worry, Manuel," Harold reassured. "The same God who has led you all your life will meet this need."

Manuel endured the five-and-one-half-hour operation on January 29, 1976. Two discs were removed and the spine was fused.

Recovering in Martin Luther Hospital, Anaheim, he was never lonely. So many associates and other friends visited him that he asked Juanita Leasure if she would please bring a guest book.

His medical expenses ran to almost $6,000. Wycliffe Associates met the need.

Associates have also provided medicines and the medical equipment for clinics related to Wycliffe's translation ministry.

Harold Leasure and his fourteen-year-old son David personally delivered an X-ray machine to a clinic in Guatemala. The machine was a gift from a Baptist church in California and had been reconditioned by one of

Harold's old sales competitors, Jim Sharp, at Radiological Equipment Assistance Program in LaVerne, California. As Harold and David were climbing to the 6000-foot level near Guatemala City, the engine stopped. Harold got out and lifted the hood. He quickly determined that the spark plug wires had overheated and shorted out.

"Can you fix it, Dad?" David asked apprehensively.

Harold shook his head. "We need a new set of wires, and I don't know where we can get them."

The chill of the high altitude was settling around them. Harold patted David on the shoulder. "Don't worry, Son. The Lord will take care of us. I don't know how, but he will. Let's pray."

Harold had just murmured "Amen" when a horn sounded behind them. They looked back to see a Chevy pickup pulling a trailer. The driver stopped and introduced himself as Claude Carey from Idaho. "We're Wycliffe Associates on our way to the Wycliffe place in Guatemala City. What's the problem?"

Harold was elated. He pointed to the wires.

"Well, the only place you can get a set of wires is back in Mexico City," Claude said. "But I just happen to have a set of extra wires for a Chevy V-8 engine in the back of my truck. They should fit your engine."

Within the hour Harold and David were rolling on with the Careys behind them. "Wow!" David exclaimed. "God really provided. If they'd been five minutes ahead of us instead of five minutes behind, we'd still be stuck back there."

Wycliffe Associates have been friends in need scores of times to Wycliffe members in distress.

The Willis Ott family's house in Bolivia was destroyed by fire. Only their linguistic research and translation materials and some of the children's clothing were salvaged. WA provided $1,200 to replace clothing, furniture, books, appliances, and other personal items. "We praise the Lord with grateful hearts for each associate who helped," the Otts wrote.

A few months later at the Wycliffe center in Colombia, a grass fire started on a neighboring farm and quickly spread. The water system, provided earlier by Wycliffe Associates, prevented a catastrophe, but Frank and Jerry Morgan's home was leveled. Replacement costs ran to over $7,000. Again WA came to the rescue.

On Christmas morning 1974 Cyclone Tracy slammed into Darwin, Australia, flattening almost every building in the city of 50,000 people. The Wycliffe center, established for work among outback aborigines, did not escape the destruction. Homes were destroyed along with the guest house, and other buildings were seriously damaged. Wycliffe Associates in the U.S. gave over $5,000 to help the Australia branch and their supporters rebuild the facilities. Included in the gifts was $1.75 from eight-year-old Ian Martin of Hemet, California. It represented more than half of his savings from allowances and work.

Two years later WA was faced with a much larger relief challenge closer to home when tiny Guatemala was hit by a disastrous earthquake that killed 23,000 people, injured 77,000, and left over a million homeless. The modern Bible translation movement had been born in Guatemala and at the time of the mammoth quake translation teams were scattered throughout the country. Fortunately, no Wycliffe members were injured, but homes and clinics received heavy damage. Some villages where Wycliffe personnel were located were virtually wiped out.

Harold Leasure organized a work caravan of twenty from Iowa and California to help. A second group from Arizona, led by Tucson Chapter Chairman Bob Seng, drove to northwest Guatemala and built a clinic from the ground up. Those in the first caravan divided into small teams and rebuilt and repaired translators' homes in three towns. Charter WA members Claude and Jerry Carey from Idaho were hard at work when the others arrived. Jerry cooked and helped wherever she was needed while Claude staked down 350 tents provided by the Canadian government. In a report Harold wrote:

Each member of the team was motivated to do as much as possible in the short time he could give. As we worked with the translators in the difficult task, there was satisfaction in our teamwork. Somehow we knew we were contributing also to the spiritual building of Guatemala and we could share their slogan: Together we are able.

Other associates contributed also. John and Jeanette Lewis from Deerfield Beach, Florida, spent eight weeks in Guatemala helping with reconstruction and repairs. Many who couldn't go contributed money. One associate who took a personal hand in raising money was Mose Gingerich, a plumber from Hartville, Ohio. Mose flew to Guatemala and filmed an on-the-scene report. Returning home, he showed the pictures in churches and raised over $2,500.

Merrilyn and her twin Merrily are thirteen-year-old daughters of Ted and Lillice Long. They were born at the Wycliffe center in Peru where the parents were told that Merrilyn had congenital kidney problems. When she was ten, doctors advised that within two years she would either have to go on a dialysis machine or have a transplant.

The day of reckoning came in the fall of 1975. Merrily was the obvious donor. Ted and Lillice prayed that she would volunteer. She did. They felt God guiding them to have the surgery done in Boston where Dr. John Merrill, a doctor who had pioneered in kidney transplants with twins, could supervise. Where they would live and how they would pay for the surgery was left in God's hands.

They radioed Lee and Edna Farnsworth in Santa Ana, California, a retired couple serving Wycliffe Associates as ham radio operators. Edna put through a phone patch to Mary Cates, editor of the WA *Newsletter* and secretary to Doug Meland, then executive vice-president of WA. Lillice summarized their situation and asked if WA could help arrange housing in the Boston area. She then gave

Mary a list of their supporting churches in Southern California. "Please give them this information and ask them to pray," she requested. "We need money too, but prayer is more important." Mary promised to contact the churches and also call Wycliffe friends in Boston.

Betty Vetterlein, sister of translator Dow Robinson and daughter of longtime Wycliffe librarian Grace Robinson, answered the phone at Park Street Church, Boston. Betty promised to do what she could.

When the Longs arrived in Boston, Betty and her husband Russell welcomed them and invited them to stay in their home for the first few weeks.

The Park Street Church had been a Wycliffe supporter for years. "Dr. Paul Toms, minister of the church, graciously informed his congregation of our needs," Lillice said in an article in the WA *Newsletter.* "What a remarkable church that is and what wonderful, sharing people. They showered us with love, fellowship, and prayer, and helped us in many ways."

Paul Bishop, a young lawyer from Park Street Church, obtained court permission for Merrily to be the donor.

Wycliffe friends all over the area pitched in. Rev. and Mrs. Brian Dixon invited the Longs to move to their home, which was nearer the hospital. Shortly before the surgery, the Longs attended a Wycliffe Associates dinner in Boston. Arthur Greenleaf, WA's northeast area director, introduced them and asked people to pray. Several offered to give blood for the girls.

On the day of the surgery, October 29, medical personnel and other workers at the hospital waited anxiously for the results. When the girls came out of surgery (Merrily at 12:30 and Merrilyn forty-five minutes later), people hugged each other in delight. Later in the day Lillice sent a joyful message to friends and loved ones around the world: "Both girls doing very well. Kidney working fine. Everybody has great peace. As far as we can tell operation 100 percent successful."

After the surgery Wycliffe friends and other believers in Boston area churches continued supporting the Longs with prayer and physical provisions. A temporary home of their own was made available and even furnished.

The home was loaned to them by Tom and Jane Yount of Oak Ridge, Tennessee. The Longs had met the Younts in Peru several months before and had become friends. Mr. Yount, a business executive, was transferred by his company to Boston, and the family bought a home there. Then they decided to remain in Tennessee. When the Younts learned that the Longs would need to live in Massachusetts for several months after the transplant, they immediately offered the use of their home.

Several months later Lillice wrote in the WA *Newsletter*:

> . . . Merrilyn and Merrily are fine. Merrilyn has gained a total of twenty pounds and grown two inches. Merrily has grown one and one-fourth inches just since December.
>
> Along with a perfect operation and recuperation, we praise the Lord for all the people he brought together to take care of our needs—from the doctors (John Merrill, Richard Wilson, and A. P. McLaughlin and their teams) to friends all over the country who have written, prayed, and given so generously. We felt you took us into your hearts and felt this with us as keenly as though we were part of your family and these were your girls going through this operation.

And the twins added notes of their own:

> Every night I thank the Lord that I am alive and well and I thank him for a wonderful sister who was willing to do this for me. And thank the Lord for you for helping and praying me through this transplant operation.
>
> Love,
> Merrilyn

I do thank the Lord I could do this for my sister and that it was 100 percent successful. Thank you for your love, gifts, and prayers.

Love,
Merrily

This was more than enough reward for what their friends and Wycliffe Associates had done.

SPECIAL PEOPLE
MEETING SPECIAL NEEDS

Thousands of lay people have provided special assistance to Wycliffe Bible Translators. While few have had roles in life-and-death dramas, all have made vital contributions.

In this chapter we look at some of these special people and what they have accomplished.

Sun Chargers for Translation Teams

Tall, husky George Campbell is an electronics engineer who learned about a special need through a ham radio contact in Peru.

From Orange, California, George picked up Paul Wyse's signal from Yarinacocha. They exchanged first names, made ham talk, and agreed to hook up again. Over the months they became quite good friends.

"We talked about our work," George recalls. "Paul told me how they were using modern technology to help the people of Amazonia. That interested me. I also sensed that Paul was happy, confident, and full of joy. But intellectually I just couldn't believe as he did."

George became so interested that he phoned Wycliffe for an application to serve as a radio technician. "I came to a question that asked about my Christian experience. I didn't have one. It made me mad because I really wanted to help."

George had attended church when he was young, but he was now quite skeptical of religion and would argue with his wife Jeannean and Christians at work. "I had a niece that died and I'd say, 'All right, where is God when a child dies? I'll believe in God when he makes the sun stop at high noon.' " He refused to let his two young children go to Sunday school "because I didn't want them brainwashed."

Then a couple of years after he began talking with Paul Wyse, something happened to change George's life. "On Father's Day, 1970, we went to a friend's house for lunch. We decided to take a dip in the pool and, since I wasn't much of a swimmer, I was the last one in. In the deep end of the pool I found myself unable to get to the surface. It was just like holding in outer space. I kept thinking maybe someone will see me. Then everything went black.

"It turned out that my son did see me lying on the bottom and got help. By the time they pulled me out, my heart had stopped. They did a chest massage and started artificial respiration. They felt there was no hope, but my wife prayed, 'O God, don't let him die.' After several minutes I started to breathe. When I finally became conscious the only thought I had was that God was real and that he loved me.

"In the hospital I developed pneumonia. My fever ran up to 104° and hovered there for days and days. I knew I was at peace with God, and I felt sure I would live, though I could tell by the faces of visitors that they didn't think I'd make it. One day one of the Christian fellows from work stopped by. 'Mike, why don't you ask the Lord to help me right now?' I asked. He prayed a very short prayer. I was healed right there. The doctor listened to my chest and had me X-rayed. He was amazed and said I could go home. The next week I was back at work."

George and Paul continued their friendship, but now they were brothers in Christ. They began discussing a new type of battery power for radios at translation locations. "When the batteries go down, the translators are cut off from the center," Paul told his California friend. "We keep a stock of big storage batteries just for that purpose, and when a team misses a couple of radio skeds we fly fresh ones out and bring the old batteries back for recharging. It's a lot of time and expense. If only we had longer lasting power."

George had designed antennae for space vehicles and was familiar with solar cells. "They're small, lightweight, and never give out," he told Paul. "I'll send one down if you'd like to test it."

Paul installed the cell and radioed back that it worked pretty well. Other Wycliffe fields learned about the new power source and requested panels.

George got a cost estimate of eighty-three dollars and talked to Wycliffe Associates, with whom he had recently become acquainted. WA made the solar cell panels a project for the month of July 1973, suggesting donations of eighty-five dollars to cover the cost and shipping charges for each cell. "Let's help 'send the light' in the form of 'sun chargers' for translation teams," the Newsletter invited. By year's end twenty-five solar panels were on their way to translators in Peru, Colombia, Papua New Guinea, the Philippines, and Mexico. Each could convert enough energy from the sun to power a two-way radio or a tape recorder indefinitely.

"Queen America" and "King Dog"

George is one of several ham operators in the U.S. who relay prayer requests and other emergency needs from the fields. For several years the hams took turns in a small radio room at WBT headquarters and later from the radio room in the new WA building, which George Campbell installed. The WA station, WA6CJB, was the command center for the WA Prayer Force Network which often had thousands praying for a single concern during a twenty-four-hour period.

The Prayer Network continues on a less organized scale with the hams now working out of their homes. Among the most active are Lee and Edna Farnsworth.

Both got their licenses after Lee retired from his job as service manager for an auto dealer. They operate off the same set, but their call letters are different. Edna's "handle" is "Queen America Ontario," representing the last three letters of WB6QAO. Lee takes a longer moniker, "Willie Baker Six Fox King Dog" for WB6FKD.

One day they were talking with a local ham friend and fellow Lutheran, Frank O'Leary. Frank, who dubbed himself "Truly Bright Underwear," kept regular skeds with Lutheran missionaries and knew about Wycliffe Associates. "George Campbell is only on for Wycliffe once a week," he told Lee and Edna. "He sure could use some help."

The Farnsworths' offer of aid was accepted with enthusiasm. For awhile they used the set at the WA office. Then, because their home equipment was more powerful and they needed to monitor long, sometimes involved communications, they resumed operation at home.

Most of the requests they handle are for phone patches to relatives and supporting churches of missionaries. Often an aged parent becomes seriously ill and a son or daughter wishes to talk to him or to a close loved one. Or, as in the case of the Longs, a missionary family wants to make arrangements for medical treatment in the U.S.

Working in shifts, Lee and Edna take Wycliffe field workers first. Then they accept as many "standbys" as time permits. One was an American serviceman from Antarctica requesting a phone patch to his mother living near the Farnsworths. Lee kept the channel open while mother and son chatted for forty-five minutes over the phone.

Lee and Edna have come to love scores of Wycliffe members they know only by voice. Because of health and financial limitations, they never expect to visit the fields. But on rare occasions they have the joy of a visit from one of their missionary friends.

"I was scrubbing the floor one day and Lee was in the garage," says Edna. "These strangers came to the door and the man said, 'Edna, do you have a few minutes?' I instantly recognized the voice of Al Townsend. He and his wife Jan were dear friends from Peru, and here we were meeting them for the first time. I called Lee and we had a lovely long visit. It was just great."

The Garageman and the Marine

Life looked pretty good for Paul Griffith when the California space industry was on the upswing. Then the industry took a nose dive and Paul was looking for work. Like thousands of other veteran space employees, Paul had a twofold handicap: he was too old (in his late fifties) and his skills too specialized for the competitive job market.

Paul had once taught automotive mechanics, so why not open his own shop? He prayed about it, then ran an ad in the paper: CHRISTIAN MECHANIC FOR AUTOMOBILE REPAIRS. HONEST WORK. YOU GET WHAT YOU PAY FOR.

Johnny Mitchell of Wycliffe Associates called. "I'll bring my car in for a tune-up and see what kind of work you do," he proposed. "Then perhaps we can send a lot of Wycliffe cars to you."

During the next couple of years Paul repaired around a hundred cars for WBT members and WA staff. He gave a special rate, cutting the price to just above his cost.

One Sunday at Calvary Church in Santa Ana, a citrus grower friend said, "Paul, I have a friend at the El Toro Marine Base who's been wanting to work on missionaries' cars. You and he should get together."

Captain Mike Morgan, his wife Carol, and three little daughters attended Calvary Church also, but because of the size of the congregation and their age difference, Paul didn't know Mike. They talked by phone and Mike came to the shop. Paul immediately liked the tall, clean-cut young Naval Academy graduate, who was head mechanic for his squadron.

With Mike working on Wycliffe cars in his spare time, they made a good team. Then Paul began having back problems and was forced to find less strenuous work. He sold the shop equipment to a friend of Mike's for half price. The friend loaned the tools back to Mike for his work on missionaries' cars.

The two men's families got together often. Since the Griffiths had no children, they talked of adopting Mike and Carol's. Then came the fateful accident. Mike was checking out the cockpit of a newly delivered plane when, for some unknown reason, the seat ejected. Mike shot through the canopy and fell back on the wing. He was rushed to the hospital, but never regained consciousness.

A Christian Marine buddy, Todd Nabors, spoke at the memorial service for Mike. "If there's a man here by the name of Charles, I'm sure he would want to know that Mike prayed for him constantly," he said. Charles was not there, but he got the message and went to see Carol.

"I used to tease Mike about Christ," he remembered painfully. "I could tell it hurt, but Mike didn't get angry. One day we were flying, checking out a plane. Mike said, 'Let's point the nose straight up and see how close we can come to heaven.' When we fell back, the pilot said, 'This is the closest we can get.' Mike's response was, 'I know Someone who can take you all the way.' That's the type of guy he was, Carol."

Charles finished his term of enlistment and went home to Wisconsin. Later he called Carol to say he had become a Christian as a result of Mike's testimony. Several more of Mike's friends made the same commitment.

The auto equipment lay unused in Mike's garage for several months. Then Paul Griffith learned through Wycliffe Associates that the auto shop in Papua New Guinea was terribly underequipped. He called the friend who had purchased the equipment for Mike. "Yes, give it to Wycliffe," he concurred.

The equipment list included a two-stage air compressor,

(above)
Bill Butler, founder
of Wycliffe Associates.

(above)
Dr. Dale Kietzman, co-founder

(center)
Uncle Cam Townsend,
founder of Wycliffe Bible
Translators

(below)
Jim Shaner, president
of Wycliffe Associates.

(below)
Dr. Rudolf A. "Rudy" Renfer,
co-founder

(above) The mark of lay involvement is everywhere at Wycliffe Associates. Ollie Carlson finishes installing the WA emblem and name plate outside WA's new office building in Orange, California.

(below) Four telephone men—"ding-a-lings for Christ," as they term themselves—pack a suitcase for a trip to the field. Left to right: Glenn German, Ed Nelson, Don Cooper, and Carl Taylor.

(*above*) Anton Willoughby, 74, helps rebuild translators' home in earthquake stricken Guatemala. Harold Leasure photo

(*below*) Associates believe in getting their hands dirty for the Lord. Jack Kendall, left, is the founder of WA's field construction department.

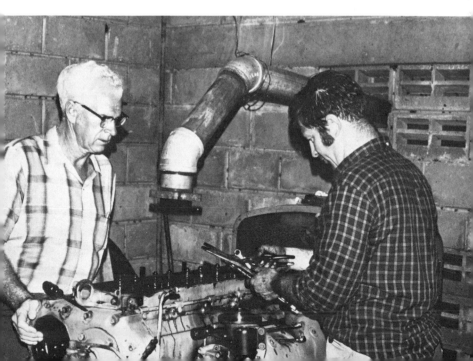

(above) Paul Doolittle makes trips to the field to repair missionaries' cars.

(below) Associate Ken Mitchell checks out Chief Yapeta from Papua New Guinea on a fire truck. Ken is public relations officer and chaplain of the Santa Ana (California) Fire Department. The chief is in the U.S. for WA dinner meetings.

(*above*) Wycliffe Associates challenges retired Christians to start a new career. The first senior citizen to respond to job listings in the WA *Newsletter* is Mrs. Lillie May Saenger, to prepare art sketches for Bible story books in Papua New Guinea.

(*below*) Dr. Wendell P. Searer, president of Christian Medical Missions, is one of many medics responding to WA's challenge for lay involvement.

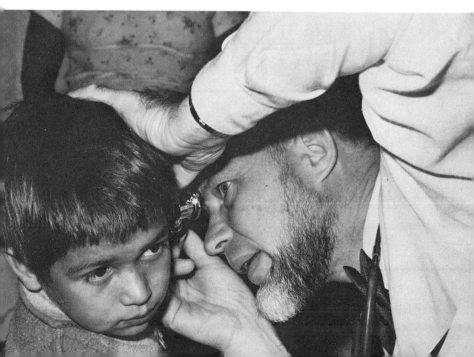

(*above*) Lee and Edna Farnsworth serve Wycliffe missionaries through their hobby of ham radio. They handle hundreds of phone patches for translators wishing to send emergency messages home. Mike Rupp photo

(*below*) Fred Chambers, 747 jet pilot, does his skydiving act for a "Missions at the Airport" crowd.

(above) Thousands of Christians know Wycliffe Associates through faith promise dinner meetings. Here George Cowan, president of Wycliffe Bible Translators, presents the Bible translation challenge to a Glendale, California, group. Mike Rupp photo

(below) Even children respond to the challenge of Bible translation and become involved.

2/12/72

Dear Friends,
Hi, I really liked the banquet tonight I hope $30 isn't to little but I think the sooner I give my money to you the sooner I'm going to heaven because we're not going till everyone knows about Jesus. Well I hope this little bit helps

your Sister
Rose Rose

P.S. Bye

Dear Gentleman or Lady,
I am only 12 years old and I get $11.00 a month to buy my clothes and tithe. But I want to give some money to Wycliffe for the missionaries, so I can only give 50¢, and I want to pray for all of you.

(above) Wycliffe Associates assists Wycliffe Bible Translators in giving God's Word to the Bibleless peoples of the world. Above, a Chuj boy in the mountains of Guatemala reads the Gospel of Mark, translated by Ken and Barbara Williams. Ken Williams photo

(below) Anyi Christians of Ivory Coast receive the first book ever printed in their language—a collection of hymns, prayers, and Bible verses. Jonathan Burmeister photo

a master motor analyzer, a distributor tester, an air jack, and other special machines and tools, plus technical manuals valued at $400. In a few days it was all crated and on its way to the Ukarumpa center, where it is now used in servicing jeeps, dump trucks, pickups, a grader, a schoolbus, and a logging truck. Wycliffe Associates paid the shipping charges.

The Amazing Paul Doolittle

You'll find Paul Doolittle in a little garage on Second Street in Santa Ana, California. If his shiny head isn't buried under the hood of a car, look for his feet sticking out from underneath. Paul is a first-class mechanic and a transplanted New Yorker who moved to the Golden State thirty years ago "because they didn't have a snow shovel that fit me in New York."

Wycliffe members are apt to say, "If Paul Doolittle can't fix your car, better sell it for junk." Paul has fixed some that were almost at that stage.

Take the old Corvair van that was given to Wycliffe back in 1964. It sat around the garage for a month until Bus Dawson came by saying he had been appointed to direct Wycliffe's pavilion at the New York World's Fair and could Paul "have it ready tomorrow. We'd like to use it at the Fair."

Paul grimaced and allowed it would take a lot of work. "If you let loose of the wheel it makes a left turn, and if you let loose of the shift it pops out of gear," Paul explained. "So what are we waiting for? Let's get the transmission out."

They rebuilt the transmission, ground the valves, put in some new bearings, and did a few other things. Bus and his colleague Tom Lyman left the next day.

They drove to New York, having to stop only in Arizona to replace the generator brushes. The van gave good service, hauling Wycliffe personnel back and forth from their lodging to the Pavilion of Two Thousand Tribes, and was returned to California still purring.

Paul repairs a good many furlough cars for Wycliffe workers and, as if this weren't enough, goes to Mexico City when branch members there come in for their annual business conference. During a month's "vacation" he may fix up to fifty vehicles, charging only for parts and taking meals with his customers. "Some of the translators are lacking in mechanical skills," he says dryly. "Or else they manage to keep their talents well concealed."

Not so with Jana Shields, a single woman who is a translator. "She mentioned that she'd like to overhaul the transmission of her International Scout and would I please supervise," Paul says. "The day we set for the job I told her to go out and get it unbolted and I'd come and lift it out for her. I thought it would take her two or three hours. About twenty minutes later she called, 'I'm ready.' I helped her get it apart and back together. But she did all the boring, lubricating, and other stuff. Better than the men."

Mission Aviation Fellowship's Dean Berto helped Paul work on cars for Wycliffe members in Mexico City during one branch conference; then the two men loaded their tools into Dean's car and started for the MAF base in southern Mexico, where Dean was to relieve a pilot for a few days. They were just sixteen miles from their destination when a landslide forced them to turn back to the nearest motel. The next morning they filled their gas tank to the brim, thinking they might have to take a long detour. All went well until Dean slowed for a curve and discovered the brakes were failing. When they finally were able to stop, they discovered the gas tank was aflame and the fire had burned the tubing carrying the critical brake fluid. There was only time to salvage essential baggage.

They got a ride to the MAF base at Ixtapa, where Paul overhauled a jeep that had been sitting in the weeds for a month. They took a ride to check it out and came upon a stalled taxi. Paul popped out with his little pliers and bent the breaker arm in the distributor to open the points.

"Now try it," he said. The Mexican driver hit the starter and drove away grinning.

The grateful MAF pilot obliged Paul by taking him along on a flight to deliver some typhoid serum to a village. When they landed, the children took one look at Paul in his jumpsuit and boots and yelled, "Astronaut! Astronaut!"

Textbooks for MKs

Ralph ("Bart") and Naomi Bartholomew are public schoolteachers in West Covina, California. Bart's brother Paul is a JAARS mechanic in Peru, and his parents worked at Wycliffe's U.S. home office after their retirement. His father Robert was on the committee that formed Wycliffe Associates.

Bart and Naomi knew about the schools Wycliffe maintains at all major centers for members' children. They knew that if it were not for the schools, many translators and support workers would have to interrupt their work and come home for their children's education.

From Paul and his family they had heard firsthand of the shortage of good textbooks and educational equipment which U.S. families take for granted. And Bart and Naomi knew there were millions of "out-of-date" texts molding away in school district warehouses in California, most of which were only five or six years old. Many had never been used. But California law said they couldn't be destroyed or given away by school personnel.

Bart taught eighth-grade science and understood that science books could quickly go out of date. But history, math, language, typing, home economics, reading, and other undated books were still usable. Many of the old ones were better than current titles, he and Naomi felt.

Couldn't something be done to make them available to Wycliffe schools abroad?

Bart talked to a Christian friend in a Kiwanis Club. "Maybe we can do something," the friend said. He found that the law permitted service clubs to use old textbooks in projects. With the backing of his fellow Kiwanians, he requested surplus books from the local district to send to mission schools. District officials replied in effect, "Come and get all you want."

Bart and Naomi sent lists of available books to every Wycliffe school and asked educators to make selections. They also sent individual copies of some books for examination.

The Bartholomews' garage and patio were jammed with books when the orders began arriving from Wycliffe members. They wrapped, boxed, and addressed the books at the house, then took them by truckloads to the post office. Unable to pay all the shipping costs, they asked Wycliffe Associates for aid. WA members contributed $1,500 to help send over 14,000 books to Wycliffe schools.

The books were sent at the right time. Two years later the law was repealed, allowing surplus books to be used in California. Quantities of books were no longer available.

Other Wycliffe Associates have also provided books. When Elener Grossman of LaPorte, Indiana, read in the WA *Newsletter* that Wycliffe needed texts in Ghana, she talked to fellow church member Dave Tucker, the manager of the local Scott, Foresman publishing plant. Dave checked surplus stock and found all the titles and number of copies needed. Within a few months the books were in the mail, courtesy of Scott, Foresman.

Fireman on Call

Ken Mitchell is a specialist in fire prevention for the Santa Ana, California, Fire Department. This lean, blue-eyed grandfather does double duty as public relations officer and chaplain of the 230-member department.

He is tops in both jobs. The fire prevention program which he directs has placed first in national competition, first in U.S. cities of the same size, and first in California. Every year during Fire Prevention Week there is a local parade of up to 2000 costumed youngsters, a soapbox derby, and a baby-sitter's clinic. Another feature is the "Careless Lawn Cemetery" at the Civic Center Plaza. Tombstones behind a white picket fence bear such inscriptions as "I struck a match to find a gas leak." And throughout the year elementary schoolteachers use a fire prevention teaching guide which Ken and the teachers developed. All this means fewer fires, lower insurance rates, and heavy demand for Ken to speak in other cities on preventing fires.

As lay chaplain for the Santa Ana Fire Department, Ken conducts funerals, counsels fire fighters and their families, writes a minisermon for the Women's Auxiliary's newspaper, and witnesses for Christ at every opportunity. Converts, some of whom are captains of stations, proudly wear small crosses and fish tie-bars.

Ken knew about Wycliffe Associates from the start. The Wycliffe headquarters in Santa Ana was just across the street from a fire station, and he was acquainted with Bill Butler through the local Christian Businessmen's Committee. His idea for helping to provide fire-fighting equipment for Wycliffe centers came after the Santa Ana Fire Department collected 90,000 Betty Crocker coupons to provide a fire engine for a small city in Alaska. "We could do the same for Wycliffe," he told Bill.

Wycliffe Associates and the Santa Ana Fire Department started a drive. Thousands upon thousands of coupons, cut and torn from cereal boxes, cake mixes, and other Betty Crocker products began arriving at the collection point, the training facility for the fire department. The Women's Auxiliary trimmed and packaged the coupons for redemption by General Mills at five dollars per thousand.

The Colombia center had already been given a refurbished U.S. Navy fire truck by the Daly City, California, Fire Department. With the new water system and hydrants installed by WA work crews, it could handle any emergency at the center.

Battery-operated portable fire pumps seemed more

practical for Papua New Guinea, Wycliffe's largest center. Much less expensive than a truck, they could be mounted on water drums and transported in a pickup truck. Amateur fire fighters could hit a grass fire quickly, before it spread to buildings. And the pumps, with their powerful hose pressure, could handle second-story flames with ease. When the fire was extinguished, the truck could be used for other jobs.

For 156,300 coupons General Mills sent a credit of $781.50, enough to purchase four of the portable fire pumps for Papua New Guinea.

Wycliffe centers in Peru, Brazil, Colombia, and the Philippines then asked for fire pumps. Peru wanted a "one-man fire department," consisting of a five-gallon tank, double action nozzle with hose, and an eighteen-inch pump which could be carried on a man's back for fighting brush and forest fires. The coupon campaign continued for another year, with a total of around 500,000 collected.

It couldn't have been done without Ken Mitchell—a fireman on fire for the Lord.

Washington Beat

About 6:30 A.M. each weekday morning two laymen leave their homes in Arlington, Virginia, and melt into the stream of suburban commuters pouring into downtown Washington, D.C.

Ed Davis heads for his office in the Pan American Building where he is liaison officer for the Organization of American States (OAS). Ed Boyer disappears into the mammoth Health, Education, and Welfare bureaucracy where he is management officer for a department.

Both men are highly skilled specialists in their respective fields. Both are active laymen in Fourth Presbyterian Church, a center for evangelical ministry in the Washington area. Both are deeply involved in helping further the goals of Wycliffe Bible Translators.

Because his father was a missionary in Cuba and Guatemala, Ed Davis grew up speaking Spanish. He flew for the U.S. Air Force in World War II, studied at the University of Southern California's School of International Relations, then went to work for the Organization of American States.

As a program manager for OAS he set up high-level meetings throughout the hemisphere, a job that required contact with foreign nationals at all levels, from elevator boys to presidents. One night in 1958 he was passing a church on the way to the Mexican National Theatre in Mexico City. "I heard singing and, having a little time to kill, decided to go in," he recalls. "I stayed for a missionary program about Bible translation started by a man named Townsend. I didn't know anything like this existed in Mexico."

The next year he was in Quito, Ecuador, to set up the eleventh annual OAS Conference. There he met Rachel Saint and several other Wycliffe members. He was impressed by their linguistic abilities, graciousness, and rapport with Ecuadorian officials. He tried to hire them but they said what they were doing was more important.

Four years later Uncle Cam went to Ed's office in Washington. "His mannerisms and easygoing ways reminded me of my father," Ed remembers. "I just loved him. I told him, 'Wycliffe has offices in other capitals. You ought to have an office here. He said he had been thinking that too, and intended to propose it to the Wycliffe board. I promised to help all I could."

The office was opened a couple of years later with the assistance of Dale Kietzman, Ben Elson, and interested laymen in the Washington area. Ed Davis and Ed Boyer were among those participating from the start.

Ed Davis's forte was diplomatic contacts. He helped Uncle Cam set up the annual Bible Translation Day ceremonies in a Senate conference room. He put him in contact with important government officials and Uncle Cam took it from there.

Ed Boyer's speciality was involving laymen, although

the other Ed helped in that category, too. Soon they had a Washington lay committee coordinating the activities of forty key persons in the Washington area.

They developed a mailing list of 3500 for a quarterly newsletter. They gave hospitality to Wycliffe members who had business or came to speak in the Washington area. They provided a book and brochure display when Wycliffe members spoke, and if a full-time Wycliffite wasn't available, they handled the program themselves.

Under Ed Boyer's leadership, the talented Washingtonians prepared a script and hired a Boston group to produce a multimedia film on Bible translation—"If Your God Is So Great." A leading reviewer called it a "breakthrough in missionary communication." Housed in a special van, partially outfitted by WA board member Lloyd Bontrager, the multimedia presentation was shown by Wycliffe teams to almost 60,000 people during a sixteen-month period. An equal number of viewers saw a single-screen version during a twelve-month period. Sixteen thousand of these viewers committed themselves to pray, give, or serve with Wycliffe.

The Washington team directed Wycliffe's attention to numerous minority languages spoken by groups that had immigrated to the United States. Many were from foreign countries "closed" to missionaries. At the urging of Ed Boyer and others, Wycliffe assigned veteran translator Dr. Esther Matteson to make a survey of these groups.

Through his government contacts, Ed was able to locate valuable surplus equipment available for use by nonprofit agencies overseas. Items from jungle hammocks to helicopters were obtained at nominal expense for Wycliffe's use.

The motto of the Washington lay supporters became: A job for every volunteer. Lay helpers typed letters and stamped envelopes to keep office expense low. Rent and staff salaries were paid entirely by the Washington group.

In 1976 a corps of computer specialists began working on Wycliffe's new SPEED (Scripture Publication Easy Edit

Development) system which is similar to the project initiated by Wycliffe Associates in Minneapolis. The Washington group is presently raising funds, locating equipment, and enlisting short-term personnel for SPEED. They expect to provide some of the twenty-five computer systems Wycliffe anticipates needing within the next three years.

Wycliffe Bible Translators now has a regional office in Washington and the lay volunteers are working in conjunction with the Wycliffe members assigned there. "We share the same goals," Ed Boyer says. "We're trying to speed the Word to the Bibleless people of the world."

These are only a few of the hundreds of special lay volunteers who are meeting special needs. If space permitted, we could tell you about . . .

—Louie Hanberg of Hillsboro, Oregon, who built a pair of unique "Jungle Bugs" to roll across the soggy terrain around Wycliffe's center in Ecuador. Made of converted old Volkswagens, and somewhat resembling a dune buggy, each Bug carries two people and 300 pounds of cargo. At Limoncocha they're used to haul everything from visitors' luggage to breeder bulls.

—Harry and Barbara Brite of Pleasant Hill, California, who took a wrong turn off the freeway in a rainstorm, lost a muffler, and were helped by a furloughing Wycliffe couple who wouldn't take money for repairs and hospitality. Fifteen months later the Brites saw a notice on their church bulletin board that someone in Wycliffe needed a microscope. Barbara called the WA office for instructions about where to send it, and soon a microscope was on its way.

—Dr. Ed and Doris Potwin, who may have traveled more miles to serve Wycliffe members than anyone else. In 1959 Ed spent several weeks at SIL in Norman, Oklahoma, giving examinations and fitting glasses at cost to WBT members. In 1962 he sold his practice in California and has been a "circuit" optometrist ever since, visiting all the SIL schools when they're in session, stopping regularly at Wycliffe's international headquarters, and traveling to Jungle Camp on his mission for better sight. While Dr. Ed tends to optometry, Doris does secretarial work, helps with children, and does whatever else she can.

The list seems endless of kind, generous folks who give of their time, talent, and treasure to facilitate the heaven-blessed work of Wycliffe Bible Translators.

GIVING A LIFT
TO JAARS

JAARS airplanes and radios opened the remote jungles and hidden mountain valleys to Bible translation. Without Jungle Aviation and Radio Service, many Wycliffe linguists could not be working in areas cut off from land routes to the outside world.

And there would likely not be a JAARS without lay involvement. From the committees that have raised funds to purchase planes, helicopters, and other equipment, to the hardy, muscular volunteers who have constructed most of the facilities at the international headquarters in Waxhaw, North Carolina, the stamp of homeland assistance is upon JAARS. Commercial pilots, electronics engineers, businessmen, carpenters, plumbers, and many others are, under God, the support of the world's most unusual airline.

"Actually there isn't much difference between the lay volunteers and our full members," says JAARS' bouncy, energetic executive director Bernie May, himself a veteran JAARS pilot. "We're all people with the same mind and motivation putting our mind and effort to the same task."

Starting from Uncle Cam's vision, JAARS had only one plane and pilot flying in one country, Peru, in 1949. Today JAARS has a full-time work force of over 400, operating sixty-nine planes and helicopters out of twenty centers and more than 300 radio stations around the world.

Waxhaw is the main center for personnel training, preparation of aircraft and other equipment, and the communications nerve center for Wycliffe operations. Because of distance and remoteness, every center abroad must carry a bank of test equipment and a large stock of parts. The combined inventory of planes, radios, engines, and other parts represents millions of dollars in contributions.

Just drop into any JAARS radio shack and the importance of lay contributions will be obvious.

Take Limoncocha, Ecuador, from which JAARS services translators in their jungle locations. Ron Durie, an avionic specialist, waves a hand at a row of steel instruments with dials and flickering needles. "Every piece of equipment is critical for our flying operations and for keeping radios at village locations functioning," he says. "Some of the instruments belong to me and other JAARS members here. We're required to have our own tools when we join. Of course, our supporters provide the funds for them. Most of the rest have been donated by lay people to meet specific needs. We couldn't operate very well without the equipment they provide.

"This voltage meter, for example, can make precise measurements of frequencies in the new aircraft radios. If a transmitter or receiver jumps off frequency, as occasionally happens, communication can be lost. In bad weather this could spell trouble. With the meter I can locate the point of error and the operator can make the adjustment.

"How did we get it? Abe Yoder, a member of a work party from Hartville, Ohio, came in and asked me what I needed. I told him I'd been praying about a voltage meter. He asked what it cost and I said about $450 or a little more. Four months later a short-term assistant in the farm program went home and came back with the meter. It actually cost $650.

"In case of a real emergency," Ron continues, "I radio Waxhaw or a friend who knows something about electronics. Just the other day I needed a tiny transistor, about an inch and a half long, for a Helio Courier radio. The plane was grounded and couldn't fly until we got it. I called Vincent Lutz in Medina, Ohio. He's a banker whose hobby is electronics. I told him what we needed. He airmailed it immediately to our office in Quito and it was sent over on the next DC-3 flight."

JAARS' largest-cost items are naturally the planes. Since JAARS, as a subsidiary of Wycliffe, has no denominational or corporate financial backer, the entire fleet represents the stewardship of concerned lay people, and Wycliffe members giving from their small allowances.

Many of the planes that fly translators in and out of their remote stations and keep them supplied are named for American cities where the funds were principally given for their purchase. The Spirit of Oregon, a single-engine Cessna, flies in the Philippines. It was purchased by faith promise gifts from the first series of Wycliffe Associates dinners.

There's a story behind the acquisition of every plane. Take the first DC-3 which went to South America to fly cargo and passengers between large cities and jungle centers.

In 1965 Nathan Bruckhart, a Mennonite builder, took several pastors from the Lancaster, Pennsylvania, area on a tour to South America. They came home eager to help Wycliffe and later started their own organization called Bible Translation and Literacy Association.

They began promoting Wycliffe in the Lancaster area. They offered scholarships, for example, to young people wishing to attend a summer SIL.

Later that year (three years before the formal birth of Wycliffe Associates) they held a faith promise dinner in Lancaster for a DC-3 and received promises of $20,000, one-third of the cost of a plane. The next year they contributed toward the purchase of a Helio Courier for Indonesia.

When Wycliffe Associates came along it was easy to

organize a WA chapter in the area. Although the Bible Translation and Literacy Association continued, some of the members also joined WA. Both groups have continued to back Wycliffe projects. In 1975 a faith promise dinner resulted in $40,000 for the purchase of two helicopters for service in Papua New Guinea.

JAARS' second DC-3 sprang from seed planted by Bernie May in a talk to the Sunday school at the First Presbyterian Church in Pittsburgh. Afterward a man came forward and introduced himself as Paul Duke, chief pilot for a steel company. "Our company has a DC-3 they're going to get rid of," he said. "Would you be interested?"

"Certainly," Bernie replied, although JAARS had no money for another plane. "Where is it?"

Paul took Bernie to see the plane at the airport. "This is the plane we need," Bernie declared. Paul promised to talk with company officials.

But they had already promised the plane to LeHigh University, which then intended to sell it. However, Bernie was so sure the Lord wanted JAARS to have this plane that he kept working to get it.

Now, having received the plane, LeHigh was unable to get its asking price of $64,000. Bernie and Lawrence Routh, then chairman of the JAARS board, went to see the member of the university board in charge of disposing of the plane. After considerable bargaining by Bernie, he agreed to accept $32,000, on terms, with the down payment of $8,000 due in two months.

Bernie didn't know where they would get the money, but he felt God wanted JAARS to have that plane. He asked his home church to pray and began giving out information to everyone who would listen.

The ball started rolling. Dr. Robert Lamont, a pastor in Pittsburgh, invited Bernie to speak to a group of businessmen. At the meeting Dr. Lamont asked for contributions for the plane and the men gave $7,000. More money was raised through a Philadelphia committee, and within six months the plane belonged to JAARS, debt free. When the plane was dedicated at the Philadelphia International Airport, over 700 persons who had helped showed up to see the plane dedicated for service in the jungles of Ecuador.

Bernie took the DC-3 to Reading, Pennsylvania, where a number of men from his home church had volunteered to pretty it up. One afternoon while they were working, a construction company executive taxied up in his personal Helio Courier. He overheard them talking about how the Lord had provided the plane and walked over and introduced himself as a fellow Christian. He was impressed to learn that JAARS was flying single-engine Helios like his own Helio No. One—the first ever made.

Six years later Bernie was back in Pennsylvania and received a call. The caller said he would like to donate his personal Helio No. One to JAARS. He didn't even want a tax receipt.

The volunteer pilots who ferry the planes to the fields, then deadhead back on commercial flights, are a breed of their own. For these veteran sky captains, whose ordinary routine is flying big passenger jets, piloting single-engine jobs and antiquated wheelhorse DC-3s over oceans, deserts, mountains, and jungles presents a special challenge. They do it gladly "unto the Lord." Most pay their own expenses.

Captain Orville Rogers has logged the most hours for JAARS. Lean and fiftyish, with a ready smile, Orville commutes from his home in Dallas to New York, where he flies DC-8 jets to major cities in South America. He is a deacon at the First Baptist Church of Dallas, where he has taught Sunday school for a quarter of a century.

Orville's knowledge of Wycliffe was "vague" before Uncle Cam came to his church in the summer of 1965. "Dr. Criswell, my pastor, recognized him in the audience and asked him to come to the front after the service in case anyone wanted to speak with him," the Braniff captain recalls. "I went down and introduced myself. We chatted a bit, then I said, 'I'm an airline pilot. Is there anything I can do to help?'

"That was all it took. Uncle Cam got me off in a corner and said, 'Orville, you volunteered and I'm going to take you up on it. We've got a plane ready to go, but the folks in Miami who were going to pay for it didn't quite meet their goal. Our policy is not to send a plane to the field that isn't paid for, so I'm wondering if you might talk to some of your pilot friends.' Uncle Cam is the world's best at convincing you he needs your help. I got together some friends and relatives and together we raised about $5,000. Then when the plane was ready, he called and asked me to ferry it to the field."

The JAARS pilots at Waxhaw checked Orville out. Then, after dedication ceremonies in Miami and Dallas, Orville climbed in the Cessna's cockpit and headed south.

He overnighted at Brownsville, Texas, then flew on to Guatemala City where he refueled. A few minutes out of the Guatemalan capital he flew into a heavy rainstorm, and had to drop below the clouds to a few hundred feet above the treetops. It was still raining when he finally reached Panama City where he refueled the third time and took off on the final uneventful leg of the flight to Bogota, Colombia.

Orville has since handled about one international ferry a year, plus making other JAARS hops within the country. His fifth ferry was very special. Beside him in the Cessna 206 bound for Brazil was his wife Esther Beth. The plane bore the name of their beloved son, Curtis, a Marine helicopter pilot killed in Vietnam in 1970.

"I'm glad to serve an organization that takes the gospel to people in the boonies who might otherwise never know," Orville says. "I think the Lord led me into aviation just so I could be of service to JAARS."

On a Cessna 206 ferry to Switzerland Orville divided flying duties with United's Bob Burdick. On one lap of 1550 miles between radio checkpoints, they saw only ice floes below. Ron Litton, a Frontier captain, and Ron Gluck of JAARS, were scheduled to take the plane on to Yaounde, Cameroon, in West Africa, but at the last minute Ron Gluck came down with a "bug" and ended up in the hospital. Ron Litton had to take it on alone.

Ron flew the single-engine Cessna straight across the Sahara with no landmarks and remained on course. The second day he had to fly 860 miles without radio contact because two stations were off the air. He eventually ended up in the dark over Africa, praying that the control tower at Yaounde's airport would not shut down. The tower stayed open and Ron landed right on course.

He reported to JAARS, "Twice on this trip I flew for hours with no navigation aids and ended up exactly on course. Very unusual—with all the clouds, rain, and rough air, there had to be wind from somewhere. The Lord was not my co-pilot, he was my captain."

Bob Burdick came to the same conclusion after a transatlantic flight en route to Nepal. Flying from North Carolina along the coast to Newfoundland, he decided to turn on his anti-icing heater. A few minutes later he noticed his compass was off thirty-five degrees from what it should have been. He knew he was not off course. He could only conclude that the heater had created a magnetic field, throwing the compass awry.

The next morning he took off over water. The ice was bad and he had to keep the device on all day and make the thirty-five-degree allowance on the compass reading. Had he not turned on that heater the day before, he would have followed the compass far off course into the North Atlantic and would likely have run out of fuel over treacherous ice.

Why do the well-paid commercial jet pilots take such long, arduous, often chancy trips? "We're following God's command to help take the gospel into all the world," says Bob Burdick. "Our lives are in his hands the minute we lift off the runway. Only he can make us successfully 'mount up with wings as eagles.' We experience the reality of Psalm 57:10: 'For thy steadfast love is great to the heavens, thy faithfulness to the clouds.' "

Ron Litton and another commercial pilot, Fred Chambers, perform skydiving acts for JAARS' "Missions at the Airport" programs. Free-falling from 10,000 feet, they crisscross in the air and land in small, marked circles while the crowd gasps in astonishment.

The affable Fred Chambers, who flies 747s for American, puts on a heart-stopping solo act.

With Bernie May at the microphone doing the color for the assembled crowd, the JAARS Helio levels off at 10,000 feet. Fred stands in the rear door and touches off a red smoke bomb. As he leaps, the people on the ground see the smoke separate from the Helio. Zooming and sailing like a descending bird, he swoops downward at 200 miles an hour. Suddenly a yellow cloud mushrooms around his feet and he whips to the left. Then in another cloud of smoke he swerves back. Finally, at 2,000 feet, his colored chute opens and he floats to a perfect landing in the tiny target area.

Since 1973 over fifty Missions at the Airport programs have been presented on Saturdays at locations ranging from modern airfields to country cow pastures. Besides skydiving, the program features Helio Courier and helicopter demonstrations and rides, voice radio contact with Wycliffe missionaries in South America, testimonies by pilots, and a Wycliffe or JAARS film every hour on the hour. Wycliffe and JAARS books and literature are also available. And there's a generous potluck lunch for everyone. Production of such a program requires ten to twelve separate lay committees, of three to seven persons each, to handle parking, bookselling, ticket selling, airplane loading, and many other jobs.

One exciting variation of Missions at the Airport is the annual September fly-in at Waxhaw when three to four hundred pilots drop in for a gala celebration. They arrive in a wide assortment of crafts ranging from sleek executive jets to World War I vintage biplanes.

An even larger crowd comes to the Chicken Barbecue held every other August at Mose Gingerich's farm in northeastern Ohio. A veteran of many work trips to Wycliffe fields, Mose planned for only 500 people the first year and had 750 show up. In 1975 he anticipated 3400 and 4300 bought "donation" tickets at $3.00 and $2.25.

Hundreds of chickens are barbecued in a 100-foot-long pit. Baked potatoes, fruit pies, and other fixins' are served with the chicken on tables spread alongside a small lake. There are singing groups and missionary speakers for entertainment and inspiration, foreign curios for inspection, and plane rides at two cents a pound (five dollars if your weight is a secret). But the big event is the skydiving act of Fred Chambers in which he lands on a quarter-acre island in the middle of the lake.

Then after all expenses have been paid, profits are divided between Wycliffe and United World Missions.

Responses from persons attending JAARS flying programs would fill a small book. Questions frequently asked by persons taking flights include: "Is this a real missionary airplane?" "Is the pilot a real, live missionary pilot?" "Is this the airplane they fly in the jungle?"

Joe Girard, the JAARS man who directed the programs for several years, notes that "we probably fly more first-time passengers than any other group except commercial airlines." He recalls one first-time rider, a frail eighty-seven-year-old grandmother who took her first ride from a farmer's private strip near Greenfield, Ohio. "The pilot, Paul Carlson from Papua New Guinea, flew her in a Helio over her old homestead, family church, and then around the countryside where she had spent her entire life. When she got back on the ground, I believe if I'd had a JAARS application blank, she would have been ready to sign up!"

Joe reports no serious mishaps in Missions at the Airport. "We were rained out only once and the program substituted for the flying that day was just of the Lord. Our team has driven to airports on other days in autos with windshield wipers going, the rain would stop and we would fly all day, and the crew would leave in autos with the windshield wipers going again that evening. Our Scripture verse from the very beginning has been Jeremiah 33:3: 'Call unto me, and I will answer thee, and show thee great and mighty things, which thou knowest not.' "

At the sprawling JAARS center near Waxhaw, North Carolina, there is more evidence of God's provision. From a rambling farmhouse and 260 acres of pasture and woodland, the base has grown to include a paved, lighted runway, two hangars, a machine shop, a storage warehouse, communications and administration buildings, a ten-room motel for overnight visitors, a recreation center for the children of JAARS members, a clinic, and a museum. On the north side of the base JAARS families are housed in their own neat, modest brick homes.

"All that we have comes from God through his people," Bernie May emphasizes. "A few individuals have made substantial memorial gifts—the communications building, for example, was made possible by the family of Frederick B. Hufnagel, Jr., but much of the center has been financed by small donations."

Bernie mentions Bob Donaldson, a jet pilot turned grocer, in the little town of Ervin, Tennessee, who put a stack of JAARS literature and a five-gallon pickle jar near his cash register. "With customers tossing coins into the 'Jar for JAARS,' Bob was able to send a check at the end of the month for $33.62. The second month the amount almost doubled. By the third month everyone in town knew about JAARS." The money bought a radio for a translation team in Guatemala.

Still, all of the money given for the facilities at Waxhaw is only a fraction of the total property valuation. The difference is made up by the materiel and labor donated.

No one has worked harder and been more faithful than Nathan Bruckhart, a Mennonite farmer from Pennsylvania. "We can't say enough about that guy and his wife,"

Bernie declares. "After helping raise money to buy planes, they came over here and said, 'We want to help you build this center.' Then they moved into a house and settled down to work. We're naming the motel after him."

Another day a Pennsylvania chicken raiser, Amon Stolfus, drove to the center and announced that he was a friend of Nathan Bruckhart's and had visited Wycliffe in Peru. After looking around the premises, he said, "You need some builders. I'll be back."

He returned with a busload of twenty-seven carpenters, painters, cement masons, and other tradesmen. They painted one building, put in the foundation for another, and poured cement for a helicopter pad. All in a week's time.

One Monday morning a plumber stopped by in his camper and introduced himself as a friend of Amon's. "My wife and I have come to stay a week," he announced. "What have you got for me to do?"

That very morning Bernie was getting ready to hire someone to install the plumbing in the new engine shop. The visitor left on Saturday and the job was done.

When the framing was up on the youth recreation building, the pastor of a nearby Presbyterian church came over. "I'll get some bricklayers from our congregation," he promised. The bricklayers brought their relatives and friends and in a couple of Saturdays the walls were up and a fireplace constructed.

When a hangar was needed to house six new planes, Associate Tony Litsie brought a work crew from near Philadelphia to put in the cement floor.

A few days later a Canadian couple stopped on their way home from Florida and had dinner with the Mays. Bernie told what Tony's group had done, adding that the Lord had also provided money to buy the sheet metal for the roof and walls. "All we need now is someone to put it up," he said.

"Well, I'm a metal builder," the Canadian declared. "I'll bring my men down and do the job."

He was as good as his word.

"I didn't ask him. He volunteered," Bernie recalls. "Just like all the rest God has sent. They're the ones who got JAARS off the ground."

NINE

MINISTERING
TO THE MISSIONARIES

Old-time Wycliffe members have bittersweet memories
about furlough years. Some had no one to meet them at
the airport and, besides experiencing reverse culture
shock, when they reached their hometown they felt almost like strangers.

Most made up their own travel itinerary for speaking in
churches, staying wherever they could on the road. The
skeleton staff at Wycliffe headquarters in California was
simply unequipped and lacked the contacts to help very
much. About the best they could do was refer furloughers
to the untrained lay representatives in various cities.

Things are better now, but the culture shock still awaits
those coming home. As Les Troyer, who recently brought
his family home from Nepal, notes: "You feel the world
has gone on and passed you by. You see kids you knew
now grown up and married and you feel a lot older. The
affluence and the inflation almost knock you over. You
don't know how you'll cope and how your kids will do.
You pray a lot and believe that God will somehow provide for the material as well as the social and psychologi-
cal needs."

When the Troyers landed in San Francisco to begin
their first furlough, colleagues Melvin and Remona Turner
had written to close friends in Oakland asking if they
would welcome the Troyers home. These friends met the
Troyers at the airport and insisted they stay at their house

a few days before going on to Ohio where Les's relatives lived.

"We slept off the fatigue, went shopping for some new clothes, and walked around town," Les says. "We were going through a residential neighborhood with beautifully manicured lawns, when I suddenly said to Madeline, 'Where are all the people?' Compared to crowded Asia where we'd been, this was like a graveyard. It took us awhile to get adjusted to things like that."

Many Wycliffe families are, of course, fortunate to have friends and relatives meet them. Some have sponsoring churches that treat them like returning celebrities, providing them a furlough home, and helping them adjust again to a technological society. But others do not fare so well.

In the summer of 1974 Wycliffe Associates initiated a "Welcome Home" program for returning Wycliffe members. Furlough information forms were sent to a group of families with furloughs coming up. Those wishing to participate in the program were asked to provide the names of sponsoring churches and friends. WA then wrote and invited them to share in the expenses of the welcome home.

The first two families to respond, Richard and Lou Hohulin and Seymour and Lois Ashley, came from the Philippines. They were met at the Los Angeles International Airport, presented with keys to cars donated for their use while on furlough, and taken to a comfortable motel near the Wycliffe headquarters for their stay in California. During the next week, area associates took them shopping, brought them up to date on recent happenings in the U.S., and took them to a doctor and a dentist who examined them free. At Wycliffe Associates headquarters they selected linens and towels and other household items from the linen closet. Then, before leaving for the respective home states, each family was handed about $1,000 for expenses from funds donated by their friends.

This service also includes a hospitality roster of WA homes where traveling missionaries may stay from one night to two weeks in cities along their route. Before beginning their trip, the missionary family receives a computer printout from WA of hosts who have offered to entertain Wycliffe members. A (fictional) sample looks like this:

AKRON

M/M HUGH HARRIMAN	TELEPHONE
210 BRISTOL DR	216 542-6867
AKRON OH 44312	
ACCOMMODATIONS—FAMILY	NO. PERSONS 7
MEALS—BREAKFAST AND DINNER	
BEDDING—PROVIDED	
LENGTH OF VISIT—3 NIGHTS	
FILE KEY—HAR003	
M/M GEORGE HOWARD	TELEPHONE
1308 HARVARD ST	216 668-8121
AKRON OH 44334	
ACCOMMODATIONS—ANY COMB.	NO. PERSONS 4
MEALS—ALL MEALS	
BEDDING—PARTLY PROVIDED	
LENGTH OF VISIT—NO LIMIT	
FILE KEY—HOW001	

An accompanying sheet instructs: "Always write or phone in advance so there is time to prepare for you or to let you know of conflicts in schedules or other problems that may prevent their entertaining you. If arriving on very short notice, don't assume that they can accommodate you."

Missionary guests are expected to offer to help with housework and expenses, accommodate their schedule to the household, not stay beyond the time limit specified, and instruct children that there is to be NO COMPLAINING about food offered to them.

Many families on the hospitality roster are longtime Wycliffe supporters. The involvement of Blair and Martha Duff of Pittsburgh runs back to 1962 when they and a few other enthusiasts had a faith promise dinner for Wycliffe at their Presbyterian church. In the years since, they have promoted JAARS projects and scheduled meetings in other churches for Wycliffe speakers. The Duffs have frequently teamed with their good friends Mr. and Mrs. Eugene Dotter in showing Wycliffe films and giving talks for Bible translation on their own.

"We have good memories of every Wycliffe member we've entertained," says Martha. Blair adds, "We've never met a Wycliffe person who wasn't dedicated and completely honest. When they leave we feel we really know them."

They remember one in particular who came to Pittsburgh before the hospitality roster was compiled. "Neil Nellis was just a name to us when he wrote from Mexico and asked if we would line up some meetings in Pittsburgh," Blair recalls. "He arrived on the bus from Texas with reservations in a seedy old downtown hotel. Gene Dotter went down to get him and persuaded him to cancel the reservations and stay at our place."

Martha picks up the story. "He carried only two suits. We sent one out to the cleaners with one of Blair's suits. The evening the suits came back, he went out to a meeting we'd scheduled and returned full of enthusiasm. The Dotters were here and Betty remarked, 'Are you sure that's your suit?' He looked down at the trouser cuffs that hung over his shoes and said, 'It does feel a bit big. Why, it isn't mine at all. I must have taken Blair's by mistake. I'm so sorry.' He was so wrapped up in his work that he hadn't even noticed what he was wearing."

Neil stayed three and a half weeks and returned to Mexico. Several months later Blair was to speak at a business conference in Mexico City, and he took Martha along. They wrote Neil of their plans to rent a car in Mexico City and drive the hundred miles out in the country to the Wycliffe translation center where the Nellises were working. When they landed at the airport, there were Neil and his wife Jane with a huge bouquet of flowers. "When they gave us the flowers," Martha says, "we felt like celebrities. And, of course, they refused to let us rent a car."

Pat and Jeanne Denham were also providing hospitality for Wycliffe families years before WA had a roster. The attractive couple live in Oklahoma City where they earn a living from a laundry business.

"Most people think Fuller Brush or Avon when they see a strange face at the door," says Jeanne. "I think Wycliffe."

The Denhams discovered Wycliffe about twenty years ago when Pat was in charge of getting speakers for their church's Wednesday evening summer picnics. "Somebody suggested that I call Turner Blount at the University of Oklahoma in Norman, where his group was training missionary linguists. Turner came and we liked him so well that we went back for more. Ken and Evelyn Pike came the next time, and after that we had Wycliffe speakers every year."

Jeanne remembers when the Wycliffe gang "invited us down. We worshiped with them in a hot gym where the sweat was pouring off everybody. I can still hear them singing, 'It Will Be Worth It All.' "

Jeanne noticed that the children of faculty and students didn't have playground equipment. "The little ones were playing in the dirt in a chicken wire enclosure. That broke our hearts. We went back and talked to some Sunday school classes. They purchased teeter-totters and swings for the children."

The concern of the Denhams and their friends led to the building of residence homes in Oklahoma City for Wycliffe teenagers who, for lack of schools, could not stay with their parents on the fields. "Wycliffe wasn't able to provide schools and children's homes then as they do now," Jeanne explains. "Many children had to stay in this country and attend school. Some didn't see their parents for a year at a time.

"That's the biggest sacrifice a missionary family can make. I've seen kids running and crying after their parents as they drove away."

The Denhams changed to another church, Metropolitan Baptist. They and other Metropolitan families frequently had Wycliffe children in their homes for meals and parties. "We thought of them as next to our own," Jeanne says. "And I guess they thought of us as second parents. I really felt for the parents so far away, sacrificing to get the Word into minority languages. We got lots of letters asking how their kids were doing. One, I remember, was spotted with tearstains."

Because of the advances in Wycliffe's educational program for members' children, there are only a dozen teens living in the residence homes today. With the smaller number and with three of their own, the Denhams are not so closely involved. But occasionally a familiar face pops up to remind them of a child they befriended in years past. "I think of Nate Waltz," muses Jeanne. "Seems as if it was only yesterday that he was here eating spaghetti. He could eat it three times a day. Now he's married to a sweet girl and they're giving God's Word to the Guanano people in Colombia. It's nice to know we had a little part in the development of his life."

The Wycliffe hospitality record is probably held by Roy and Martha Long of Fort Lauderdale, Florida. They average around 400 Wycliffe overnight guests a year. In 1975 they played host and hostess to 523.

They meet some of their guests at the Miami International Airport where Roy, a pilot with thirty-five years' flying experience, is based with Eastern Airlines. His present assignment is training other pilots to fly the giant Lockheed L-1011s.

"When we started meeting Wycliffe people back in 1968," Martha remembers, "we frequently didn't know what the new arrivals looked like. We had only their names and perhaps the number of children. And they didn't know what we looked like. We'd stand outside the door to customs, asking people coming out if they were the ones we were to meet. Sometimes we'd ask five or six before we got the right ones. Then we began wearing SIL badges and they'd recognize us. I've seen some break into tears."

Roger and Ruth Alder and their three children were

new Wycliffe members coming from Australia for training at JAARS. Roger called from the airport. "Have you got your baggage off yet?" Martha asked. "We're all through and ready to go," he replied in his broad "down under" accent. "Good," she replied. "Look for me in a brown Oldsmobile."

When she arrived he looked at the car and looked at their baggage and said, "Oh, we'll never get it all in."

"Well, we can try," Martha said. They did, and off they went.

Later the Longs were at JAARS in Waxhaw and ran into the Alders. Roger shouted to a friend, "Here's the woman who literally scooped us up off the deck in the Everglades."

Because Miami is the major port of entry from South America, Wycliffe has a shipping office there. Dan and Rosie Doyle take all the overnight Wycliffites they can accommodate. The overflow goes to the Longs.

Some South American airports do not have night operations; therefore, planes often arrive in Miami at night and depart in the early morning hours. Old Wycliffe friends (those who have been to the Longs' at least once) frequently can get a car at the Wycliffe office and drive out to Fort Lauderdale. "We leave a key where they can find it, fill the towel racks in the hall bathroom, and go on to bed," Martha says. "They can even take a swim in the indoor pool if they wish."

A plaque before the mirror in one of the guest bedrooms speaks the sentiments of Roy and Martha:

Guests, you are welcome here;
Be at your ease.
Get up when you're ready;
Go to bed when you please.
Happy to share with you such as we've got;
The leaks in the roof and the soup in the pot.
You don't have to thank us or laugh at our jokes;
Set deep and come often;
You're one of the folks.

Roy and Martha's guests have included Wycliffe members from every South American country, and Aucas on tour with Rachel Saint. Their most regular guests are the DC-3 crews who make flights to the U.S. every three months. When a crew must stay over a weekend, they attend the Longs' church. If Roy happens to be flying, Martha takes them. A friend has told her, "When I need to find you in church, I always look for a pew with one woman and a row of men—'Ma Barker' and her 'boys.'"

The Longs' home is filled with jungle artifacts and other gifts from their Wycliffe friends. Their living room is like a curio shop with wood carvings, spears, blowguns, fishnets, jaguar teeth, a leather chair, and many other items. One of their most precious keepsakes is an alpaca rug embroidered with the design of the L-1011 plane that Roy flies for Eastern. It came from Wycliffe friends in Bolivia.

Wycliffe members in Ecuador have made Roy and Martha "honorary members" of their branch, "in recognition and appreciation of gracious hospitality, for the demonstration of loving concern, and for their fellowship in this work of the Lord." The tribute was painted on sheepskin and framed for presentation to the Longs.

"When we visited Ecuador, the whole gang turned out to greet us," Martha reports. "They treated us like royalty."

From Quito they flew in the DC-3 over the Andes to Limoncocha, where a smaller plane took them to translation locations. "Landing on a 'gash in the woods,' a strip almost as wide as it is long, was a new experience for me," Roy recalls. "It's like putting your car in the garage at forty miles an hour. But I wasn't too apprehensive. Those JAARS pilots are the best."

Roy and Martha are actively involved in the Fort Lauderdale Wycliffe Associates Chapter. The chapter was organized by WA area director Stan Shaw as a follow-up of a rally with Rachel Saint. The sixty-plus members promote a Wycliffe project each month. One month they bought sheets and blankets. Another month they purchased mattresses for the Wycliffe children's home in Bolivia.

Every year they have a faith promise dinner for around 300 Wycliffe friends. Martha is the reservation secretary.

And it was only nine years ago that the Longs were introduced to Wycliffe by a former pastor who had been Bernie May's college roommate. Roy had just been transferred from New York to Miami and they had moved into a new house. "Only one of our three children was still at home, and we wondered what we were going to do with this large house," Martha says. "Now we know."

With Wycliffe's membership now over 3500, about 500 members are always on furlough, along with others traveling and speaking on special assignment. More and more are using the WA hospitality roster in planning their trips.

Dr. Esther Matteson travels to universities around the country searching for speakers of languages native to areas closed to missionaries. She discovered at the International Institute of Detroit a professor who was born in Tarsus, birthplace of the Apostle Paul, and came to the U.S. as a refugee from Armenia, which is now under Soviet control. Dr. Robert Rubyan spoke two Armenian dialects, one of which had been targeted by Wycliffe for Bible translation. He immediately promised to help Esther translate Scripture into that dialect.

On a cross-country trip from Washington, D.C., to California in late November, Esther stopped in Iowa, where she spent a night with Marilyn Schlenker, widow of a JAARS pilot killed in an accident while on furlough. Leaving Iowa, she drove southwest, where a family on the hospitality roster was expecting her. Realizing she would be late arriving at their home, she called ahead. The man gave her directions and said, "We'll be waiting up."

He was standing on the curb in the dark when she arrived. Inside were his wife, son-in-law, daughter, and grandchildren.

"The children want to meet a real missionary," the grandmother said. "Could you possibly tell them a story before they go to bed?"

Esther is never too tired to talk about the Piros of Peru,

for whom she helped translate the New Testament. She told about their names for various star constellations—the Anteater, the Turtle, the Crocodile's Chin, and the Jaguar's Chin—and about their interesting names for animals and plants. "They have a tiny white gourd they call 'the mouse's gourd.' And they have a vine they speak of as 'the turtle stairway,' " she informed her rapt audience.

Then she told how she arrived in the Piro village to find two chiefs, White Condor and Antlers, searching for God. "They looked at the stars and knew there had to be a God. But they didn't know who he was and if he had ever spoken. God helped me and my co-workers to write down in their language what God had said.

"Do you know what God said? He said that he sent his Son to be our Savior. The Piros believed that and, my, how their lives were changed."

It was past eleven when the mother pulled the children away and insisted that since they had now seen and heard a real missionary, it was time to go to bed.

Paul and Grace Bartholomew were reluctant to use the hospitality roster when they arrived in Miami on a furlough vacation trip. They felt that a family of eight just wouldn't be welcome.

"Then God impressed on us that the people on the hospitality list had signed up because they actually wanted Wycliffe folks to visit, relax with them, and share about their work. So out came the list," Paul says.

The first family lived in Pensacola, Florida. Paul called the man, but still couldn't bring himself to ask for accommodations. "Uh, do you know, Sir, where a missionary family of eight might spend the night in the Pensacola area?" he finally asked.

"Stay here," the friendly voice invited.

They did and were treated as if they were doing the host family a big favor.

They drove northwest to Yellowstone Park, stopping at other hospitality homes along the way. They had no names to call in the park and, after sleeping in a rustic but cold cabin, wondered how far they'd have to drive before finding a motel.

They reached the exit and stopped to hand the park ranger their toll ticket. "Where are you from?" he asked.

"Oh, if I told you, you'd be confused," Paul said.

"Confuse me," the ranger insisted.

"We're from Peru, South America. We work with Wycliffe . . ."

" . . . Bible Translators," the ranger finished. "Do you know Paul Marsteller?"

"Sure do," Paul replied. "We went to language school with Paul and Mary in Lima and worked together for five years."

"What's your destination tonight?" he asked.

Paul explained that they were going down the road a ways until they found a motel.

"No good!" he objected. "You come over to our place. We have a trailer and a tent out back for the kids, sleeping bags all over. My wife will be glad to see you."

They had a great time. They went canoeing and hiking and the ranger's wife showed them through the park. Then as they were getting in the car, she asked, "How do we get on this Wycliffe Associates hospitality roster?"

Steve and Judy Van Rooy had a different experience. They were driving across Montana when their VW camper's engine began sounding off. Steve pulled to the side of the road and made a quick check. He determined, to his despair, that the bearings in the generator had burned out, causing the engine to overheat.

Judy checked the hospitality roster. "There's a family back in Miles City," she said. "Maybe they will help us."

The young couple hitchhiked back to Miles City and called the Delbert Bosckis residence. Mrs. Bosckis answered the phone. When Steve told her what had happened, she chuckled. Steve didn't think it funny. Later he learned that a few days before, another couple had called Delbert with the same problem.

Delbert came and picked them up. That afternoon they

went out with another roster host, Nathan Miller, to bring in the van. Evening was approaching and Delbert asked if they'd like to attend the service at their church. When the Van Rooys said yes, he asked if they'd give their testimonies and show slides. Again they smiled assent. Delbert quickly called the pastor, and the Wycliffe couple became the program for the evening service.

After a good night's rest, Delbert, Nathan, and Steve attended to the repairs, and the Van Rooys were again on their way.

Ministering to missionaries on the fields is another story. Traditionally, missionaries have been idealized as super-saints who heroically serve in difficult places. Missionaries are still admired, but there is growing recognition that they, like other Christians, have deep spiritual needs. Consequently, pastors and lay church leaders in the homeland are making personal field visits to minister to the missionaries they help support.

Rev. Homer Kandel is pastor of Countryside Chapel and also a storekeeper in north-central Ohio. In 1976 his church of less than 200 members supported in part over a hundred missionaries from faith promise receipts of $144,000.

Homer is one of a number of pastors and Bible teachers who conduct services at Wycliffe bases. These services are held in conjunction with annual branch conferences. "I go both to learn and to minister," the Ohio pastor notes. "They share with me what God is doing through them in their villages and I share with them a pastor's understanding of God's Word."

Homeland pastors usually spend from three to seven days preaching and counseling at a center. But after his first visit to the Wycliffe group at Lomalinda, Colombia, Rev. Tony Gould of Jackson, Michigan, decided a week wasn't enough. "I'm going to bring my family and stay longer next time," he told the missionaries.

His church board gave unanimous approval to an indefinite leave of absence. They would pay a supply preacher for Sundays, the assistant pastor would handle the Wednesday evening services; the deacons would do the hospital visitation. "We'll all benefit from your going," a board member said.

On Sunday evening before their scheduled Tuesday departure in February 1976, the church held a farewell service. One deacon read a poem written for the occasion. Another outfitted the pastor and his family with a used tube of toothpaste and a bar of soap with a hole in it. Then, turning from the humorous, the entire congregation joined hands and encircled the Goulds. Tony prayed, "Just as we are enclosed within their hands, O Lord, so may you keep a hedge around us."

The Goulds—Tony, Sharon, and their three children, Debby, Stephanie, and Andy—arrived at Lomalinda on Friday and settled into the house of a Wycliffe family that was away in their village. Tony preached two sermons that first Sunday. On Monday the children began attending classes with the Wycliffe children at the Lomalinda school, a plan worked out with their home school before leaving.

"I want to be your pastor for the next few weeks," Tony told the Wycliffe members of the Colombia branch. "I want to visit in your homes and pray with you just as your pastor does at home."

Every day Tony circulated about the base on a borrowed Honda, stopping briefly at the printshop, the hangar, the radio shack, and other places where Wycliffe personnel were at work. In the evenings he and Sharon visited in homes. Sharon helped in the school library each weekday morning, served in the kitchen at night, and made herself available as a pastor's wife.

After three weeks of getting to know Pastor Tony and his family, the missionaries began opening up and coming to him with their problems. One translator cried as he admitted, "I don't want to go back to my village. I don't like the bugs, the thatched roof, and the isolation. But God put me there and I'll stay."

The last week of the Goulds' visit was marked by a spiritual renewal that swept across the center. Veteran missionaries praised God for his cleansing, renewing power and thanked the Goulds for coming.

Altogether the Goulds spent six weeks at Lomalinda. Each week they mailed home a tape to keep their church informed. The church secretary, who was staying in their house, sent them tapes of the services. Just before Easter Tony went to the radio shack and called a ham friend in Indiana who made a phone patch to the secretary. She taped the message and it was played to the congregation after the Easter cantata.

The Goulds visited two language groups during their seventh and final week in Colombia. On the last Sunday they shared in a communion service with Christians from the jungles. One of the believers told Tony, "How honored we are for you to take communion with us." Tony replied, "No, it is we who are honored to be with you."

After a day of shopping in Bogota, they flew home. The pastoral visit was so meaningful that Tony is now trying to enlist other pastors who will go and minister for four to six weeks at a Wycliffe center. "They need us and we need them," he declares.

Another pioneer mission to missionaries resulted from Wycliffe Associates asking Pastor George Munzing of Trinity United Presbyterian Church in Santa Ana, California, to make a pastoral tour of WBT centers in South America. The church had just granted George a five-month sabbatical for study, travel, and rest. He accepted the offer gladly.

Two members of the church staff and a church elder agreed to join him on the mission. He would be the leader and preacher; Paula Carson, Trinity's director of children's education, would work with children and single women; Dave Hansen, a senior collegian and junior high director at the church, would interact with teens, and insurance executive Roger Tompkins, the church elder and a teacher of teens, would minister in youth-parent relationships and serve as business manager for the team. Wycliffe Associates paid Pastor Munzing's expenses, church friends provided for the two young staffers, and Roger paid his own fare.

They touched down first at Bogota on April 17, 1975, and were met by Trinity members Chuck and Lolly Alexander. (It was a visit they would treasure, for the following August the young missionary wife died from a brain tumor.)

Then they were off to Lomalinda, and from there to centers in Peru and Brazil. They spent an intensive three to five days at each center, holding evening meetings for all Wycliffe personnel, leading daytime discussions on the Christian life, and holding personal consultations in between. Their overall emphasis was on "building up the body of Christ."

Roger kept a personal journal of the trip. A sample of his impressions:

Lomalinda, Colombia
Wycliffe is interesting—run as a democracy—electing its leaders. All self-supported. Yet with all that, there are all the spiritual and personal needs of any small group of 200-300 people. These are magnified by the isolation.

We pray for the power of the Lord to manifest itself in what we do.

Missionaries aren't "super-Christians," but are supremely committed and dedicated. None of us has all the answers, but each of us has all the questions.

Yarinacocha, Peru
Our group becomes more a family all the time.

Paula is the most emotionally involved with everything. Sometimes hard for her to summarize her thoughts involved with singleness. Really feels the needs of "single girl teams"—translators who work in villages in teams.

Dave, age twenty-two, continues to surprise us with depth of insight and observation. Very quiet. Needs time for himself. *Good* with young people. Very patient.

George shows leadership strength. Draws from us and calls upon us, enjoys everything, is spiritually very mature. Providing leadership.

I've developed a reputation for summarizing and conciseness. We kid a lot about "one-liners" —homilies, proverbs, and the like.

Visit to a village—impressions: hot, sticky, mosquitoes, poverty. But with it all, caught glimpse of reality of trying to better conditions.

We left Colombia wondering how the Lord would work, as we knew no one in Peru. We leave Peru thanking him for blessing us with new friends and using us in our ministry.

Brasilia, Brazil

A very heavy time [before arriving]. Prayer for each other and for our ministry in Brasilia. We thought through the implications of an urban setting, [Wycliffe] people in apartments, us in the guest house, the pressure on the high school kids in the American School setting. We prayed hard for insight and the moving of the Spirit in our efforts here.

Sunday evening session—a high point. Real crescendo. George spoke powerfully on "Who do you say that I am?" Commitment message. Lots of kids in room. God answered prayer.

God . . . gave us insight. Used us to sensitize both adults and kids to need for adults to lead and kids to respond in building bridges of communication for reconciliation and ministry.

Belem, Brazil
Paula had a great session with the women at the center—a couple of hours. She brings a unique ministry of openness and concern. One of the women talked about the masks we all wear— Margaret had read Ortlund's comments on the ministry to each other in the Body of Christ— evidently the Lord is working with the people here, especially the women, on this subject.

I'm reconvinced at each step that none of these people are super-Christian, but all are dedicated to what they're doing . . . Although I don't feel called to reorder my life, to become a WBT missionary, I'm impressed with the commitment and the tenacity of the people, and with the nobleness of their task. What could have a more profound impact on a people than to have, for the first time, their own language written and the Scriptures in it?

For my own part, I intend to:
   Expand my knowledge and understanding of
      the Wycliffe-SIL system.
   Be open to the Lord as to what role, if any,
      he may have for me in interaction with
      WBT people.
   Try to keep up contacts with some of the
      wonderful people we met—as they come
      on furlough as well as by correspondence.
   Encourage others to accept calls to minister,
      if the Lord opens the door, to WBT people,
      wherever they are.

Reflecting on the experience, George Munzing calls it "the best three weeks of my life. It gave me a growing appreciation of Wycliffe, a whole broader, deeper vision of what missions are and the struggles missionaries go through. Our team developed a closeness as we sensed, as perhaps never before, the wonders of Christ and the unity of his Body. Beyond that we had a chance to touch lives of dear, committed people who are often hurting and in need of a word of consolation and encouragement and hope."

George Munzing is only one of hundreds, at home and on the field, who are ministering to missionaries. In so doing, they are helping build up the whole Body of Christ.

TEN

NOT RETIRED, JUST RECYCLED

When the founder of Wycliffe Bible Translators began his missionary career, average life expectancy for U.S. citizens averaged 53.9 years. Today, an American can expect to live, on the average, seventy-two years. And those now retiring at sixty-five can anticipate, on the average, being around for over fifteen more years.

More than twenty-one million are now alive past sixty-five. Most are retired from regular jobs. Many are widowed and living alone. Only a small percentage are physical invalids, unable to perform meaningful work.

The senior years are supposed to be the golden years. Yet a national survey sponsored by the Institute of Life Insurance found 48 percent of those polled agreeing with the statement: "Retirement often makes a person feel useless."

The hundreds of active, energetic, and optimistic "keen-agers" serving the cause of Bible translation will disagree.

Through the years many retired people have worked at the WBT and WA offices in Southern California. Until his fatal heart attack, Floyd Wroughton, chairman of the WA chapter in Springfield, Illinois, came each winter to assist in the WA office. One of his many jobs was preparing the posters for the Auca Update Rallies.

Mrs. Grace Robinson already had a family interest when she began helping. Her son, Dr. Dow Robinson, and his wife Lois are translators for the Highland Puebla Nahuatl people of Mexico. When Dow, Sr., retired from his career as a metallurgist in Massachusetts, they came to California. She became librarian at the Wycliffe headquarters. After Dow passed away in 1967, she continued in the library.

Don Smith came to Wycliffe as a veteran postal employee. Having once helped his dad on a route in ranching territory, he knew the postal business from ponies to modern jets. "I tried a 'sit-down' retirement, but six months was all I could stand," he says. "I found a little book in a Christian bookstore called *How to Serve God in Retirement*. The author, Paul Travis, listed a number of Christian organizations that welcomed retirees. Wycliffe was my first choice. So I went down and asked if they needed somebody in the mailroom. They said yes, and I had a job."

Don worked a year, then had to drop out for a couple of months for health reasons. His next job was with Wycliffe Associates assisting full-time WA staffer Roger Petrey.

Don's experience in handling foreign mail was invaluable, since WA sends many packages overseas. He wrapped every package with loving care. One, he remembers, was a large box of used eyeglasses for shipment by boat to Papua New Guinea. The package arrived in good shape, with not a single lens broken.

"My wife and I have no children, and very few family members left," Don notes. "Wycliffe has become our family. I've never been with such wonderful people. They help us anytime we need anything. When we're hospitalized, they're right there, just like brothers and sisters."

Harry Whitney, seventy-three, lovingly keeps the lawn and the plants and shrubs around the WA building in trim. "We have juniper, bird of paradise, begonias, camellias, azaleas, and lots more," he says proudly. "We keep something blooming the year 'round.

"My wife Dorothy and I met some Wycliffe Associates in our church, and they invited us to join them at WA for a work party," Harry recalls. "When we got there the WA people asked me about doing some gardening. I've been at it ever since. I'm happy to help out."

John Powell, a sales executive for Crown-Zellerbach Paper Company, was introduced to Wycliffe in 1958 by a surgeon friend, Dr. Ralph Byron. John and his wife Darline began supporting Don and Nadine Burns in Peru and, at their first opportunity, paid their missionaries a visit.

"We went to their schools up in the Andes, where we saw Quechua children who had not possessed pencil and paper two years before, now reading and writing," John remembers. The teachers were selected by their villages and sent to the training school at Ayacucho where the Burnses lived. Then they went back to teach the three Rs along with the Scriptures in their native language. We returned home sold on the Wycliffe product."

When Wycliffe Associates was organized, the Powells led one of the first tour groups to Mexico. "We took sixty-eight people. The trip gave them a greater sense of what Wycliffe is doing and made Wycliffe members aware of the potential of Wycliffe Associates for recruiting lay supporters."

Dale Kietzman was a member of the Powells' church, Lake Avenue Congregational in Pasadena, California. He and John frequently talked about the objectives of WA. Both concluded that the full-time WA area directors strung out across the United States, were spread too thin to be of much help to Wycliffe members on furlough. Dale and John came up with the idea of training 200 key laymen who would serve furloughing missionaries in their own localities. When a Wycliffe member was going to be in a certain area, the "keyman" in that section would be notified. He would find the missionary family a place to live, schedule meetings, arrange for an automobile, and even arrange for medical and dental services, if needed.

The keyman would also show churches how they could participate in the Bible translation program.

"When you retire, will you help us prepare keyman training materials?" Dale asked John. He promised he would.

In 1972 John stepped down from his job. During the next eighteen months he spent two or three days every week working on the keyman program. He outlined what keymen would do. He prepared manuals they could follow step by step in making the best use of missionaries' time. And he worked hard at persuading Wycliffe members to utilize the services of the keymen.

As the program developed, it seemed best to relate the keymen to WBT regional directors instead of to WA area directors. This transition is now complete.

"I'm gratified that I could contribute something," the retired sales executive says. "I'm not an evangelist. But I can set up programs, prepare manuals, and train salesmen for Wycliffe."

Retired people serve at other Wycliffe facilities in the U.S. Mrs. Verda Goff, a great-grandmother, served at the International Linguistics Center in Dallas. Her family first became aware of Wycliffe through young people going out as translators from their church in San Gabriel, California. She and her husband subsequently became prayer and financial supporters of a Wycliffe family in the Philippines.

After his death in 1966, Mrs. Goff covenanted with the Lord that when she retired and was self-supporting she would serve him full time. So upon retirement from McDonnel Douglas in Long Beach, she applied to Wycliffe.

She hoped to go to Colombia or Peru, but Bus Dawson, then vice-president for international development, said guest helpers were needed at Dallas. She sent Dr. Frank Robbins a resume of her work experience and he immediately invited her to come. "I was so thrilled and excited, I had trouble getting to sleep that night," she recalls. "I wouldn't trade that experience for any sum of money, because I knew I was where the Lord wanted me. I praise him every day for opening that door of service."

Ed Radin, a peppy five-foot-four, seventy-six-year-old grandfather serving at JAARS, feels the same way. A veteran communications expert and globe-trotting adviser to foreign governments, Ed ran into Wycliffe in Bolivia when he was sixty-two years old.

"My crew was making a feasibility study of communications for the country and I needed to charter a plane to send a couple of fellows back in the jungle," he says. "The Peace Corps referred me to Joel Warkentin with JAARS. When I called, Joel said, 'Sure, come over and bring your wife to dinner this evening.' Just like that. He'd never seen or heard of us before. From that sprang a friendship with him and his family and our long relationship with Wycliffe."

Joel was impressed when he learned about Ed's extensive experience in communications from Africa to Brazil. When Ed said Bolivia would be his last job before retiring, Joel immediately wrote Jack Kendall. Jack replied by asking Ed to help install the new telephone system at Wycliffe's center in Peru. Ed happily consented.

Back in the U.S. Ed helped Jack, Charlie Miller, Jim Keller, Jim Henderson, and other associates to locate and get in shape telephone exchanges and other equipment for Wycliffe centers elsewhere. For the most part, Ed worked at JAARS, but he did make another trip back to Bolivia to install a phone system at Wycliffe's center there.

In 1967 Ed became concerned about the need of housing for JAARS personnel around the center at Waxhaw. He and his wife Ruby bought thirty wooded acres adjacent to the JAARS property. They subdivided the land and offered lots to Wycliffe members and retired workers at a minimum cost of $500 each. Streets were opened and attractive residential homes began springing up. In tribute to the Radins, JAARS personnel named the first street Radin Road.

The Radins live today in a trim, red brick house a few hundred feet from Uncle Cam and Elaine Townsend, who also built in the subdivision. Appropriately, at the end of the Radins' driveway stands a red telephone booth.

Ruby Radin stays busy with her flowers while Ed works on communications equipment donated to Wycliffe. His heart "isn't so good," she says, and he "longs for a couple of telephone men to take things apart and catalog equipment needed on the fields. We have to sell lots of stuff for junk because there's nobody to handle it."

"But I'll keep working as long as I can hold out," he adds. "I've had meaningful jobs, but this is the best of all."

Retiree Ann Eliza Tate, a tall, stately southern lady from an old Charlotte family, lives next door to the Radins. Her husband was a prominent merchant who served as vice-chairman of Billy Graham's 1958 crusade in Charlotte. Billy Graham introduced Uncle Cam to Bill Tate, and Bill then introduced the Wycliffe founder to merchant Henderson Belk, who gave land for the JAARS center.

Bill Tate's interest in Wycliffe remained strong until his death in 1965. Afterward Ann Eliza accompanied the Townsends to Colombia. "They put me to work cleaning the library," she recalls. "I removed the books, some of which had cockroaches in them, then painted the shelves with insect repellent. It was a messy job but I enjoyed the opportunity to help the translators."

Upon returning from Colombia, she went with Elaine Townsend to the Soviet Union, where they visited linguistic minority groups in the Caucasus Mountains. In 1972 she moved to the JAARS center.

"I've been wanting to go to Papua New Guinea for two years," she says, "but my doctor says I have borderline glaucoma and should stay home for regular checkups. So I keep myself available here at JAARS."

Wycliffe Associates' policy from the beginning has been to encourage retired Christians to serve where they are most needed as their health permits.

The first to apply for a job listed in the WA *Newsletter* was Mrs. Lillie May Saenger, a sixty-five-year-old artist from Texas. Dr. Rudolf Renfer, then chairman of the WA board, sent published samples of her artwork to several Wycliffe branches, asking if they could use her talent.

Papua New Guinea responded immediately, and in a few days she was on her way. Branch director Al Pence warned that she might need three weeks to adjust to the climate and culture change. But the evening she arrived, she accepted her first assignment—to prepare ten sketches on the life of Abraham for Old Testament stories in the Washkuk language.

She completed the Abraham sketches and stayed to finish a second series on the life of Noah. Then she took home an assignment for sketches on the life of Joseph.

Over the years scores of retired associates have found adventure and fulfillment through short terms of service on Wycliffe fields. Because of Mexico's nearness and its 100-plus dialects in which Wycliffe works, many have gone there.

Ed Karsten, a commercial artist, and his wife Sylvia, a typist (seventy-nine and seventy-six respectively), have spent six months during each of the past nine years helping in the Mexico branch headquarters. After hearing a Wycliffe speaker at Trinity Methodist Church in Chicago, Sylvia started their yearly trek when she visited Mexico and typed Dr. Bob Longacre's Trique translation. She continued to type for Wycliffe members and also entertain children and help in the library. Ed designed covers and title pages for translations and other literature published by the Mexico branch.

"Gran Gran" Rich went to visit her son Rolland and his family in Peru. After the second trip to "visit the kids," she decided to remain "as long as the Lord gives me health." Though past eighty, she developed into an excellent proofreader in the Publications Department, relieving translators of much tedious work.

Elizabeth Cudney was considerably younger when she went to Peru after being widowed at fifty-one. She managed the Lima Group House for almost twenty years before "retiring" to help in less demanding work. Hundreds of Wycliffe members, associates, and other guests have enjoyed Mrs. Cudney's hospitality in Lima, the City of Kings.

After nearly half a century of practicing medicine in the Atlanta area, Dr. Charles Cunningham at seventy-two went to direct the clinic at Lomalinda, Colombia, so that Wycliffe's beloved Dr. Kenneth Altig could take a year's furlough. He treated hundreds of people—Wycliffe members, tribespeople, and Spanish-speaking Colombians from the surrounding area—and instructed translators in remote villages by radio. "The real medicine of life is Christ in us," he often said.

After completing almost a year, Dr. Cunningham had to return home because of illness. Eight months later he succumbed to cancer and entered into the presence of the Great Physician.

Dr. Cunningham's nurse in Colombia, Helen Gibbs, is also a retiree. She continues helping Dr. Altig, a longtime friend from Long Beach, California.

How Helen and her husband Harry went to Lomalinda makes an interesting story. They became acquainted with Wycliffe when Ted and Lillice Long and their children were attending their church during furlough. When Wycliffe Associates was established, Helen and Harry became charter members.

The next year Dr. Altig was home on furlough. One day Harry came to his office as a patient. "You'd better tell Dr. Altig good-bye," the nurse told Harry. "He's going back to South America."

During the examination Dr. Altig mentioned that he needed a clinic built at Lomalinda. "I'm a construction man," Harry answered. "Would you like me to come and build your clinic?"

"Sure," the Wycliffe medic responded, without knowing how serious Harry was.

Harry went home and talked to Helen. "You can be his nurse." Helen liked the idea, but it was so sudden.

The next Sunday Harry told everyone at church, "We're

going to Colombia to help Doc." Helen took her impulsive husband aside. "I think there's a little more to this than just saying we're going," she cautioned. "We should get approval from Wycliffe."

They did the necessary paperwork, and in June 1969 flew to Bogota. When they reached Lomalinda, Harry was ready to begin building, but the base director said, "Harry, I read your file. You were a chef for fifteen years and we really need a dining room supervisor. We can get someone else to build the clinic."

Harry would have to coordinate the work of seven nationals in the kitchen and purchase food from the neighboring town of Puerto Lleras—and he didn't speak Spanish. But he agreed to take the job, and despite language deficiencies, their ministry has multiplied, both at the center and among the people in Puerto Lleras.

Harry started one of his Colombian suppliers off in the bakery business, designing his oven and giving him a recipe for bread. He now has three shops, two for making bread and one for making clothing. When he offered Harry a partnership, Harry replied, "No, I didn't come to make money. I came to serve the Lord."

Harry also taught a butcher how to cut meat, and got the local farmers to raise chickens, tomatoes, and green beans for sale to the Wycliffe center. He also helped local Colombians to get two public schools going. They wanted to name one after their gringo friend, but Harry insisted they honor a Colombian.

At the dining hall Harry would personally greet visitors. One newcomer, a professor whom Harry and Helen had in their home, turned out to be an investigator sent by the government in response to rumors that the Wycliffe workers were CIA agents in disguise. He was so warmed by the Gibbses' hospitality that he invited them to visit his home on their next trip to Bogota. They did and became close friends. Their children now call Helen *Nona* (grandmother) and Harry *Nono* (grandfather).

Another professor whom the Gibbses befriended told

them, "We want Americans like you in Colombia. You really care for people."

Harry's health has deteriorated in recent years. In 1974 he had to have two major operations, and in 1976 he began receiving radiation treatments for cancer.

Still merry and smiling, the white-haired Lomalinda chef declares, "We intend to stay as long as the Lord will let us."

eleven

INNOCENTS ABROAD

Margi Brothers, an attractive brunette nurse at famed City of Hope Hospital in Duarte, California, was talking with her close friend Faith Mercado. "I've been on two short-term missions to South America with Practical Missionary Training," she noted. "Lately I've been thinking about another trip."

Faith, a widowed Christian broadcaster, remarked, "My daughter Carolyn Waltz is with Wycliffe in Colombia. I know Bill Butler, the head of Wycliffe's lay division. Do you mind if I ask him to send you information?"

Margi agreed. But by the time a packet of materials came, she had decided she couldn't leave her aged parents.

Meanwhile, an urgent request had come to Wycliffe Associates for short-term nursing help in Ecuador. A terrible polio epidemic had swept the Auca area. Fourteen were already dead. The crippled survivors were being moved to the HCJB mission hospital at Shell Mera. Two were critically ill and needed nursing care around the clock.

Bettie Butler made a quick check of the files to see what nurses had previously volunteered. She came across Faith Mercado's inquiry for Margi and passed it to Bill. He noted that Margi hadn't responded to the information previously sent and started to hand the file back.

Then he told Bettie, "Maybe she's the one the Lord wants. Let's send her a special delivery letter."

Margi got the letter December 12, 1969, when she came home from caring for children critically ill with leukemia. She had already heard about the epidemic and now read Bill's plea: "Urgently need two nurses to relieve the missionaries. Please pray about serving. Wycliffe Associates will help with travel costs, but you should be prepared to pay your room and board."

She immediately called Faith. "What do you think?"

"Ask the Lord, not me," Faith responded.

Margi prayed for guidance. She also mentioned the request to a friend at work, who happened not to be a Christian. "Well, if this is what God wants, you should do it," the nurse advised.

She called Faith to say she was going. Faith made an appeal over the radio. Margi's mother heard her name and dropped her iron in shock. Margi hadn't planned to tell her parents until all plans were made.

Disappointment came when Margi asked her boss for a leave of absence. "You'll have to resign," the director of nursing informed her. "And I can't guarantee you'll get your job back."

Margi had already decided she would resign when Faith called to report a promised gift of $500 for her expenses. After that the blessings began falling like rain. Her parents gave their consent. "Don't worry," her dad assured. "God will take care of us." Then on the only day she had to get her visa, the Ecuadorian consulate was closed, but there "just happened" to be a man in the office who gave it to her immediately. She got her round of shots —typhoid, yellow fever, tetanus, smallpox, cholera, and a polio booster in record time, and Dr. Ralph Byron at City of Hope Hospital gave her a supply of antibiotics for the stricken Aucas.

The rough going for Margi Brothers began when she arrived in Ecuador. The telegram asking Wycliffe personnel to meet her at the airport had left out her first name. They came looking for "brothers," two males. She had to take a taxi alone to the guest house. The next day she flew in the DC-3 across the Andes, but bad weather prevented a landing at Shell Mera. Back in Quito she took a bus over treacherous mountain roads that snaked around precipitous cliffs and through deep gorges. The driver recklessly bounced around dangerous curves while her stomach did flip-flops, but she found comfort in Faith's reminder at their parting: "So many things have worked out, Margi. God must really want you to go."

She reached the hospital exhausted, and after a night's rest began her first shift of caring for the two critically ill patients, Enae and Nanka. Enae was in danger of choking to death, despite a tracheotomy. She would become frightened and increase her secretions. Gurgling and choking, she would panic and cry like a pitiful child. Several times Margi thought she was gone.

Nanka was paralyzed from the waist down, but despite his paralysis he was happy and gregarious.

At City of Hope Margi had worked with dying patients, but she could talk to them. With the two Aucas she could only smile, gesture, and touch, and wait for the daily radio sked from Rachel Saint, who had remained in the Auca village with the less seriously ill.

Back in California another Wycliffe friend was making plans to help with the Aucas—Ellsworth "Bud" Swanson, forty-eight, and father of six. Bud, a physical therapist, had two medical missionary brothers, Dr. Doug, with Wycliffe in Peru, and Dr. Wally, with HCJB in Ecuador. Wally had written Bud:

> We're left with sixteen patients with varying degrees of paralysis . . . Now that the acute disease is over, these rehab problems are really serious, especially in this primitive culture. Previously an Auca that became an invalid probably would have been left to starve or been killed in a raid by enemies when he couldn't flee. Now the people

have to be taught to help these invalids survive.
It will take Christ's love to see this realized, but
God is able.

Bud's first job in 1949 had been in a polio hospital.
Since then the disease had practically been conquered in
the U.S. by the Salk vaccine. He began searching old
medical journals for instructions. In February he flew to
Quito and joined a radio conference between Wally and
Rachel in the Auca village and the nurses at Shell Mera
and Limoncocha. They decided it would be best to fly
nine stricken Aucas still in the village and two critically
ill ones at Shell Mera to Limoncocha. Dr. Swanson had
kept the nine Aucas alive in the village with a hammock
apparatus that worked like a teeter-totter, moving their
diaphragms up and down to keep them breathing. Rachel
Saint and nurse Lois Pederson had been rocking them
around the clock.

Carpenters at Limoncocha built a long thatched-roof
house similar to what the Aucas were accustomed to in
their village. In one end they put the rehab center with
two treatment tables and strung hammocks for the patients in the other.

On one treatment table Bud placed a smooth board on
which a patient could push his leg back and forth on a
skate. As his muscles became stronger, little lead bags
were added to the skate. Bud had brought equipment from
the U.S. and rigged up a system of pulleys with nylon
ropes for exercise. He also used a muscle stimulator to
help muscles contract and regain their nerve connections.

Bud spent most of his six weeks at the base setting up
the equipment and training Wycliffe personnel, Margi, and
another short-term nurse, Ruth Ann Reed, to keep the
therapy going. Margi remained three months before returning home.

She continued to pray for her Auca friends, especially
Enae and Nanka. Enae almost fully recovered and became
a Christian and a language assistant to the translators.

Nanka, who never walked again, became depressed and developed painful, running bed sores and died.

Bud returned to his group practice. Margi got her old job back, then later returned to Ecuador to help at the Limoncocha clinic again, remaining eight months before coming home to care for her sick mother. In January 1974 Margi had surgery for a malignant tumor on her leg. The following September she developed another malignancy and endured radical surgery under one arm. One of the operating room nurses told her afterward that she had accepted Christ because of Margi's testimony.

Margi's father, now a widower, is an invalid; and Margi's own health is uncertain. Still she "would like to go back for another short term. I feel God has used my life. I want to keep serving him every way I can."

Margi and Bud are just two of hundreds of guest helpers and short-term assistants (the official classifications) who are assisting full-time Wycliffe workers. Though their temporary service may not be as dramatic as Margi's and Bud's, they go in the same spirit, responding to needs. They serve as typists, secretaries, bookkeepers, radio operators, teachers, librarians, printers, artists, community development workers, mechanics, pilots, group house managers, children's home parents, maintenance men, construction workers, and in many other ways.

Guest helpers stay from a few weeks to a few months. Approval is needed from the Wycliffe branch where they wish to serve. They are expected to be in good health and of good character and to pay all their expenses. Guest helpers are students, senior citizens, and others who can be on the field for only a brief time.

Short-term assistants stay from six months to five years. STAs apply by filling out a preliminary questionnaire obtained from the WBT office in Huntington Beach, California. If the information on the questionnaire looks promising, the office contacts branches which might be able to use the designated skills. If a branch responds positively, the office then sends application papers. The forms ask for basic family and health information, signature to a doctrinal statement, and personal references. The WBT Personnel Committee, after approval, makes an assignment and suggests the length of service, usually one or two years. This may be renewed by the branch leadership up to five years without further Personnel Committee action. STAs, like career Wycliffe members, must raise funds for outfitting, transportation, and support. Not infrequently a volunteer will go as a guest helper and then after a time of service on the field, apply for STA status. Some end up joining Wycliffe.

Short-term service has been included in the policy of major mission organizations for little more than a decade. Before 1960 most missions sought only career workers. Wycliffe was a leader in showing that short terms are practical, even preferable in instances where job needs are temporary or where a candidate wishes to serve a trial period before making a lifetime commitment.

Since its beginning Wycliffe Associates has publicized and promoted short-term opportunities and assisted volunteers in applying to Wycliffe. For awhile almost every *Newsletter* cited temporary job openings requiring specific skills.

WA staffers talked up short-term openings at dinners and rallies. Scores of eager lay persons, who never realized before that they could have a personal part in mission service, asked, "Where do I write for more information?"

WA's work is only part of the short-term picture with Wycliffe. Many have heard about opportunities to serve directly from Wycliffe members on furlough and through other Wycliffe channels.

The extent of STA service in Wycliffe is revealed by a count of personnel on various Wycliffe fields. In 1977 the Philippine branch had 230 members and 30 STAs. The ratio in Peru was 206 to 7; in Bolivia, 95 to 23; in Colombia-Panama, 212 to 33. These figures do not include guest helpers.

To mention a few individuals: Dr. Arthur Lown, director of the Atlanta public schools' Reader Service for the Blind, and coordinator of the School Services for Visually Impaired Children in Atlanta was leader of his local WA chapter when he and his wife Inez were challenged to give three months to Wycliffe as guest helpers in Colombia. At the Lomalinda center, Inez, a nurse, helped in the clinic while Dr. Lown served as a radio operator.

After their service in Colombia the Lowns were accepted as STAs in the Philippines, where they now manage the nineteen-room guest house in Manila. Dr. Lown also serves as Wycliffe's Manila coordinator, which involves everything from shipping goods and scheduling flights, to overseeing the transcription into braille of the Gospel of John in Tagalog, the Philippine national language. Visitors are amazed at Dr. Lown's versatility, and when they discover he is totally blind, they marvel. "We're happy to be here to help free translators so they can give God's Word to a Bibleless group," he says.

Eileen LeGood is a red-haired, apple-cheeked English girl who was challenged by a Wycliffe member from her church in Kent, just outside London.

After Dr. Katherine Barnwell had given a talk, Eileen said, "I've been praying for you, Katy. Your work must truly be interesting and fulfilling."

"Do you want to know more?" the linguist questioned. "You could write for information."

Eileen did and was invited to spend a weekend at Horsley's Green, the Wycliffe center in England. She went, enjoyed it, and returned a second time. On the way home she kept feeling a pull toward Wycliffe. "But I like my job, and my daddy needs me," she argued. She was a senior technician in the nuclear physics section of a college. Her mother had died just three years before and she was living with her seventy-five-year-old father.

Having decided that it wasn't practical to volunteer for missionary service, she walked in to church one Sunday to hear the vicar ask, "Who will go for us?" By the end of the sermon, she was convinced that the Lord did want her.

Eileen worried about her father's response. But when she told him of her desire, he merely said, "If that's what you want, go on. I'll manage the house by myself."

She applied as an STA. Her job experience had included a stint as chauffeur for members of Parliament, including the Prime Minister. But since Wycliffe didn't need a chauffeur, she was accepted for a one-year term as a lab technician in Colombia.

When she entered the clinic at Lomalinda and introduced herself to Dr. Altig, the overworked medic grunted, "Glad to have you," and pointed to a man lying on a couch. "See if you can help him. I'll be with you in a moment."

Blood was pouring from a deep cut on his leg. Eileen quickly ripped away the trouser and began trying to stop the bleeding. She had the bleeding under control and was cleaning the wound when Dr. Altig finished with his other patient. He looked at her work with approval. "You've got a strong stomach. I need you in the office."

By the time she had settled into her room, the plucky Englishwoman had three jobs—doctor's assistant, pharmacist, and lab technician.

Looking back on her colorful life, Eileen, like many other short-termers, admits, "I never thought I'd be a missionary. But things began to happen when I said, 'Yes, Lord.' And here I am."

TWELVE

ECUADOR'S ENERGIZERS

How important are guest helpers and STAs to the operation of a Wycliffe branch?

To answer this question, we will look closely at Ecuador.

The small Nevada-sized nation boasts sparkling ocean beaches, snowcapped mountains, lush jungles, and haunting highland plateaus. It is a land of intriguing contrasts where sandaled Quichuas, with faces leathered from mountain winds, trudge along the streets of modern cities, stopping to gaze curiously into department store windows that feature the latest fashions from New York and Paris. Of the seven million citizens, 40 percent are Indian, 40 percent mixed blood, 10 percent black, and only 10 percent are of direct Spanish descent.

In 1952 the national Ministry of Education invited SIL to provide educational aid for the country's multilingual minorities. From offices and a guest house in Quito and a jungle center at Limoncocha, Wycliffe works with eight language groups—Aucas, Cayapas, Cofans, Colorados, Secoyas, Jivaros, and Lowland and Highland Quichuas. Wycliffe aid involves language analysis, compilation of dictionaries and lexicons, translation of books of "high moral value" (Christian Scriptures, citizenship manuals, health guides, and basic educational texts), and preparation of scientific papers for the academic community. Wycliffe is further commissioned to train minority teachers for bilingual schools and develop Indian agriculturists and health promoters.

The multifaceted personnel force required to meet these assignments includes linguists, agriculturists, educators, anthropologists, pilots, mechanics, nurses, artists, office workers, maintenance men, and administrators. The 1977 prayer directory listed for Ecuador seventy-three full-time Wycliffe members and nineteen STAs. The several guest helpers were not listed.

We'll start in Quito, the capital, at the attractive rectangular two-story guest house, which looks like a small motel. Wycliffe members on business or just stopping over, Wycliffe Associates tour groups, and other friends stay here for brief periods. One section houses high-school-age children whose parents are at the Limoncocha center or in the tribes. They attend Alliance Academy in Quito, a Christian school for missionaries' children.

Dave and Dorothy Yoder from Ohio are the host and hostess. Their work is much like the operators of a stateside motel with a small restaurant attached. They take reservations, check guests in and out and see that they are comfortable, supervise local hired help, and buy groceries at the market twice weekly.

Back in Ohio, Dave and Dorothy ran a flourishing Christian bookstore and helped support a missionary. Gene Zacharias, a Wycliffe member, was visiting with the Yoders in 1970 and asked them to "pray that the Lord would send a printer to Ecuador." Dave was a printer by trade, so he and Dorothy began praying about going themselves.

They needed more equipment for their store and decided to bid on some at an estate sale. When their bid was rejected, they took it as a sign to put their store up for sale. Seven prospects came in the first week, and the store was sold.

They applied as STAs and were accepted. They went first to Colombia for two weeks' training, then to Ecuador where Dave helps with printing and manages the guest house.

Dorothy's parents, Pastor Abe and Katie Miller, visited

them in Quito. Two weeks after returning home, Pastor Miller died of a heart attack. "Come and be with us, Mother," the Yoders invited.

Katie Miller is with them today, sewing, cleaning, baking, baby-sitting, and being the resident grandma. Occasionally she helps at the Alliance Academy kindergarten, and when Dave and Dorothy are away, she takes over the guest house.

"The Lord has brought me here to be with my children and grandchildren. And he's given me plenty to do," she says. "As a pastor's wife, I learned to be hospitable. We took folks in after church in the evenings for fellowship when we had only a big kettle of chili soup and sandwiches. We always had a good time singing and being together. That's the way it is here. Friends come from all over. We've had many letters from Wycliffe Associates and others thanking us for hospitality and saying they want to come back."

The SIL business offices in Quito are a short walk from the guest house. Here short-termers assist Wycliffe leaders in all capacities.

Roselyn Snively prepares art sketches for bilingual Bible storybooks, readers, math books, health manuals, and other publications. Her husband Bob is the jack-of-all-trades maintenance man and mechanic for Wycliffe vehicles. Before applying as STAs, they were active Wycliffe Associates in Grand Rapids, Michigan.

For authenticity in her drawings, Roselyn visits tribes where translators work. "It's important that the illustrations be correct," she emphasizes. "The children catch any deviation."

Roselyn works closely with Jeanne Eichelberger, an STA bilingual secretary who types manuscripts in both Spanish and tribal languages. Jeanne comes from a small town in Montana where she learned about Wycliffe through an Inter-Varsity Christian Fellowship group at the college she attended. She and her sister first decided to be STAs together, then her sister got married. Jeanne resigned her job in a bank loan department and went on alone. Her Inter-Varsity friends pledged a large share of her support.

Jeanne shares an apartment with STA Bonnie Grey-danus, a young single woman from Michigan, who teaches seventh and eighth grade English at Alliance Academy. Another single STA, Dorcas Winfrey, teaches home economics at the Christian school which is cooperatively staffed by missionary teachers.

Jeanne came for a year and decided to stay two, because "I've gotten involved here." She was surprised at the number of Americans living in Quito, the modernization of the city, and the up-to-date equipment in the office. "I didn't expect to have an electric typewriter," she says.

Jeanne and her STA roommate attend the English Fellowship Church in Quito where Jeanne teaches second-grade children. They belong to a Christian singles club which Dorcas started at the church. "I really feel I belong here," Jeanne says.

Two other single STAs, Linda Leversedge, a secretary, and Marc De Bruyne, a bookkeeper, help in the Quito office.

Don and Nadine Burns, specialists in bilingual education, introduced Linda to Wycliffe. "When I was fourteen they came to my church in Cincinnati and visited in our home. Don took time to play Scrabble and talk with me. I never lost interest in missions after that."

Linda worked awhile for a publishing firm in New York City as an advertising and editorial assistant. In Quito she is branch director John Lindskoog's secretary. She teaches a Sunday school class of eighth-grade girls at the English Fellowship Church.

"I've gotten a more realistic and practical view of missions," she affirms. "I work regular office hours and have a life-style not too different from what I would have in the States. I've learned patience here. If something doesn't get done, the world doesn't end. Everything goes on and I have a better appreciation of how the Body of Christ functions and how we can minister to each other."

Marc, a handsome six-foot-four native of Colorado, first heard of Wycliffe when WBT President George Cowan spoke to his Christian commune. "We were operating a 100-acre farm to raise money for missions," Marc recalls. "Mr. Cowan explained that Wycliffe was not trying to replace or warp the cultures of minority people, but was giving them the Word and allowing the Holy Spirit to work within the cultures. That impressed me."

Later a Wycliffe Associate came by and showed a film and distributed brochures to the group, telling how they might serve. Marc felt the Lord leading him to complete his degree in accounting. A couple of months before graduation he was cleaning out his desk and came across a Wycliffe pamphlet. Remembering the film and George Cowan's talk, he decided to write for information on short-term service.

He was shocked to learn he had to raise his own support. But he went ahead and applied and worked to save money for travel and living expenses.

Marc is now cashier in the SIL office. He makes currency exchanges, handles members' debits and credits, prepares checks for national employees, and pays local bills. As he would in the U.S., he uses a desk computer and adding machine in figuring accounts.

He lives with a young Ecuadorian pastor in the back of a church, eats Ecuadorian food, participates in the services, and accompanies the church youth group on mission trips to highland villages.

"I'm just glad to have the opportunity to serve," declares Marc.

Len and Caroline Buntz feel that way too. At fifty-seven, Len is the "old man" of the Ecuadorian STAs. Because of his flight experience, he shares the rare distinction of being an STA pilot for JAARS.

Len is now on his third career. He retired the first time

after twenty years in the Navy, then retired again after fifteen years of flight instruction for the Federal Aviation Agency.

Len and Caroline are from Oklahoma City, where they were active in the Metropolitan Baptist Church, Campus Crusade for Christ, and Wycliffe Associates. As a WA keyman, Len showed Wycliffe films and set up appointments for Wycliffe members in area churches.

They were also on the WA hospitality roster and kept a "missionary boutique" ("We didn't like the name 'missionary barrel,'" says Caroline) in their garage. Every summer they took clothes donated by Wycliffe friends to SIL at the University of Oklahoma, where missionaries could select their choices.

In the late sixties Len was an instructor for International Civil Aviation in Mexico City. Working with foreign pilots wasn't new, since he had taught scores of internationals in Oklahoma City. While in Mexico, Caroline signed up as guest helper and cooked at the local Wycliffe headquarters. Here she helped Vola Griste find the doctors in the U.S. who performed ear surgery on the little Otomi girl, Elena (see chapter 6).

When Len decided to retire the second time, he asked Bernie May, "Where can JAARS use me?" "Bolivia and Ecuador need you the most," Bernie replied. "Take your choice." Len and Caroline chose to live in Ecuador where their sons George and John could attend Alliance Academy. Their daughter Carol was ready for college.

From Quito Len and a regular JAARS pilot provide DC-3 round-trip service twice weekly to Limoncocha, taking turns in the pilot and co-pilot seats. They also make several special flights a year, flying bilingual teacher trainees to the center and ferrying cattle and other cargo to village locations. "Sometimes it's like flying a 'Noah's ark,'" Len quips. "The teachers bring along turtles, birds, chickens, small animals, anything they can get on the plane. Everything's supposed to be caged or tied down, but occasionally something gets loose. Once a macaw got into the cockpit and was about to take a peck at the pilot's ear when Bill Eddy, our mechanic and cabin steward, took care of it with a broom."

Len is an expert in navigation and aerial maneuvers. But even he will concede that flying in Ecuador is "tricky." The Quito airport is over a mile high in a valley surrounded by towering mountains, with housing developments on all sides. Branch director John Lindskoog jokingly calls a Catholic Church near the end of the main runway "Our Lady of the Last Approach."

Landing on the grassy strip at Limoncocha is even more tricky. "We come in very, very slowly and touch down almost at stall speed," Len explains. "That's because we can't apply the brakes on the wet grass. We warn everybody planning to land there. One fellow (not a JAARS pilot) thought it was no strain and put down too fast. He had to ground loop the plane to keep from going into the lake that's just beyond the end of the runway."

Caroline doesn't have a regular job, but helps out where she can. Her assignments have ranged from stuffing prayer letters for Wycliffe members to living among the Aucas as a temporary partner for Dr. Catherine Peeke.

The Aucas greeted her with curiosity at first. She had to stand with her mouth open about ten minutes while they circled her, looking at her teeth. "Most of the Aucas have just one tooth or only a stub left," she explains. She didn't feel "one bit of fear" in the village and knew that she belonged when a group stopped outside the house one day. A newcomer pointed at her and asked, "Who's that stranger?" "Oh, that's just Caroline," came the reply.

At home in Quito, Len and Caroline and their two boys live in a three-bedroom apartment (rent $180 per month) with a parrot, "Sammy Padilla," and a monkey, "Gimo." Both are gifts from the Aucas. The parrot speaks Auca well and is slowly learning English.

Locally grown fruits and vegetables are cheap. A dozen bananas cost a quarter. Len can buy a whole stalk in the jungle for sixty cents. Milk is only eighteen cents a quart.

American imports are much more costly. A box of corn-flakes costs $1.70; a tiny bottle of maraschino cherries, $2.00.

They can walk to the English-speaking First Baptist Church where Len teaches an adult class. Caroline is also active in the Quito Christian Women's Club which draws a monthly attendance of about 200.

Len enjoys canoeing down fast rivers and mountain climbing. Once at 16,000 feet he came upon another climber who said he was from Harrison, Arkansas, about thirty miles from where Len grew up. "I could pursue my hobbies back home," Len says. "The adventure and the exotic attractions aren't why we're here. We came to help the missionaries."

Limoncocha is a far cry from bustling, cosmopolitan Quito. There are no roads into the center, and boat travelers must detour off the turbulent Napo River which flows southeastward into the Maranon, a major tributary of the Amazon. Most visitors come in by air and land on the slice of green cleared from thick jungle. Limon (pronounced leeMOAN), is situated atop the bank of a spring-fed lake populated with fish weighing up to 500 pounds.

Despite the remoteness and the wetness (there are only two seasons, wet and very wet), Limon has become a favorite spot for scientific researchers to visit. Anthropologists come to study the ethnic groups in the area. Horticulturists delight over the verdant foliage and exotic wild flowers. Biologists are fascinated by the varieties of insects (one couple has spent seven years studying the army ants native to the center). Ornithologists are attracted by the variety of bird life; over 500 species have been catalogued.

For Wycliffe members in Ecuador, Limon is central to language and translation work, flying, communications, training of bilingual teachers, and development of a model farm. They have modest homes at the center along with a dining room and limited dorm facilities for transients, classrooms for teacher training, a commissary, clinic, sawmill, power plant, school for the children from kindergarten through eighth grade, telephone exchange, radio shack and tower, hangar and airfield, and small assembly building for group meetings and worship services.

Translators live at the center only part time. Support personnel, except for vacations and furloughs, are there year round. Short-termers serve as furlough and vacation replacements and fill special support jobs for which full members are not available.

Here are capsulized profiles on six short-termers at Limon:

At the hangar is Galen Wiest, a slim, carefree farm youth from California's San Joaquin Valley. Galen heard of Wycliffe from Peru translators Wesley and Eva Thiesen when they were on furlough. After finishing a junior college mechanics course, he asked JAARS if they could use an assistant mechanic somewhere. JAARS said yes and sent the standard questionnaire for guest helpers. Then they invited him to Waxhaw for two weeks of orientation before OKing him for Ecuador.

Galen works on airplane engines under the supervision of regular JAARS personnel. He enjoys the work and loves the jungle, but realizes he must have more education. He'll be returning home for Bible school training shortly "if the Lord continues to lead that way."

Judy Nordaas, from Minneapolis, is secretary to JAARS' chief of aviation in Ecuador, Roy Gleason. Besides writing letters and typing up logs and schedules, Judy keeps in contact with JAARS planes, relaying weather reports radioed in from jungle stations to the base radio operator. As if this weren't enough, she teaches physical education and coaches track and swimming at the school for members' children.

Judy was challenged by a speaker at a Navigators conference for singles. "What will you be doing for the Lord in ten years?" An STA who had taught at the Yarinacocha school for two years encouraged her to write to Wycliffe. She did and applied for STA service. Once accepted, she resigned her job as secretary in the U.S. Department of Agriculture in Minneapolis and went to Ecuador.

She "loves" her airy, well-ventilated office with a huge flight map on one wall and a display of tribal spears before her desk. She doesn't "feel isolated at all," has been to Quito five or six times in the last year, and has flown to Peru and Colombia for vacations.

She likes the casual life-style, dashing about on a Honda, wearing tennis shoes or sandals, or going barefoot if she chooses. But most of all she likes "the satisfaction of being helpful, of knowing I have a small part in helping translators put God's Word in the language and life of people who have never had it."

Guest helper Glenda Dobbs is bustling about in the base dining room, seeing that food is ready and places set for workers who will not go home for lunch and the passengers due to arrive on the DC-3 from Quito. "Everything fresh has to be washed in hot water," she says. "Even the grapefruit, oranges, bananas, and papayas from the fruit trees around the base. Gotta watch out for the amoebas and other little peskies, you know."

Glenda is praying about a missionary career. She's taking a few months off from the University of Tennessee at Chattanooga where she's majoring in special education "to see what missionary life is all about."

A jovial, outgoing young woman, she was referred to Wycliffe by a Lutheran missionary speaking at her church in Chattanooga. She put on her questionnaire that she was experienced in office work and in fast food restaurants. "I reckon they needed me to supervise the dining room more than work in an office," she says.

Before she left home, friends kidded her that she would be living in a hut in a jungle clearing. "It isn't that primitive here," she laughs, "but then this isn't the Holiday Inn either. Hot water is very limited. However, the cold showers help keep me awake."

The clinic where guest helper Sue Foster works is just a few steps from the dining room. Sue is subbing for her close friend Lois Pederson, who is spending three months on leave in the U.S. Sue, Lois, and Verla Cooper, the other Wycliffe nurse at Limon, are all from Seattle. "About a hundred of us are in a group that prays for Lois, Verlie, and two other Wycliffe members, Patricia Kelley, who works with the Aucas, and Mary Sargent, who's assigned to bilingual education here," Sue says. "I'd planned to take a trip to Africa when Lois wrote they needed help. They say, 'old nurses never die, they just volunteer.' Well, here I am.

"We see a lot of minority children dying of malnutrition. Often parents don't bring them here until there's very little we can do. It's heartbreaking. So different from what we see at home."

Sue steps into the next room and Verla mentions that the guest helper has been director of nursing for the Boeing Company's far-flung operations. "But you'd never know she's such an important person by talking to her."

Another guest "sub" at Limon is Holton Knisely who is handling maintenance for full-time member Bill Anders. Holton and his wife Mildred are living in Bill and Mary Anders' house for four months. "We wrote Bill and asked if we could help." Holton says. "He turned the work over to us."

The Kniselys are from southeastern Michigan where Bill took early retirement from his business of manufacturing automatic screw machines for the automotive industry. At Limon he keeps the electric generators and other power equipment purring. Mildred handles the bookkeeping for the maintenance department and does "lots of sewing."

"We like the food and the warm climate," Holton says. "But we enjoy the Wycliffe people the most. They love the Lord and each other. And they're much better educated than I thought missionaries would be."

The sixth short-termer at Limon is an STA teacher. A

friendly, drawling Texan, Judy McKee teaches in the school for Wycliffe children. "They're normal kids and my routine is about the same as at home," she reports. "Except they have jungle pets and may on occasion bring a snake to class. That doesn't bother me, though. I like it here."

That seems to be the common sentiment of all the short-termers in Ecuador. Several of the younger ones are seriously considering a career with Wycliffe. That isn't surprising, for within the Wycliffe membership are many short-term alumni.

As Russ Reinert (handicapped by blindness) wrote for the Wycliffe publication, *In Other Words*, "I was once an STA myself... I wanted to see if missionary life was something I could handle... Two years on the field convinced me this was where I belonged. Now I'm a full member, serving as director's assistant for personnel in Peru, and loving every aspect of the job."

THIRTEEN

CONTINUING ON TARGET

We have caught the vision, felt the heartbeat, and sensed the burden of Wycliffe Associates lay people as they assist Wycliffe Bible Translators in translating God's Word into the languages of ethnic minorities around the world. Now we must meet a few of the dedicated WA staffers and board members who keep the organization running smoothly.

From the president to the volunteers who come in to help send out special mailings, the WA staff acts as a team, each person cooperating to get the job done.

"We aren't overstaffed," says business manager Dale Herr, "so we have to give 100 percent and sometimes a little more. But the overall goal is well defined, and when we receive word that another New Testament has come off the press out in Papua New Guinea, or somewhere in Africa, or in the Philippines or Peru, it's thrilling to know we had a part in it."

In President Jim Shaner's office, bookshelves display a number of New Testaments completed by Wycliffe personnel. "It's only a part of the total number," Jim explains. "From Wycliffe's beginning until 1976, some sixty-seven New Testaments were published, but of course many more were in progress and nearing completion. With the coming of computers, manuscript preparation was speeded up considerably and New Testaments are being dedicated regularly."

Jim is a comparative newcomer to the WA staff. When Bill Butler resigned in 1975 to head up Christian Resource Management (a new organization offering professional management and promotional aid to small missionary enterprises), WA was without a president for a year. To fill the gap, the board asked chairman Rey Johnson to serve as president until they could appoint a new leader. Douglas Meland, business manager, was named executive vice-president and became the top administrator.

Rey Johnson and his wife Margie are longtime friends and supporters of Wycliffe. During the year Rey filled in as president, he gave unselfishly of his time, leaving his business for hours on end to assist at the office, attend meetings, or do public relations work for WA. He was among the early board members and served as treasurer before being elected chairman of the board. Thoughtfulness, generosity, and firmness of purpose characterized Rey's efforts on behalf of Wycliffe.

Doug Meland, a veteran Wycliffe translator and field administrator, came to WA in 1969, after finishing his work in Brazil. He was second to none in dedication to the Wycliffe goal. While the board looked for a new president, Doug kept the office running efficiently and the WA field programs moving ahead. The burden was heavy. He often worked after the regular office hours had ended. At times he enrolled in night courses that enabled him to better implement the programs of a growing organization. One was in bookkeeping, another in salesmanship, and another in computer operation and programming. As business manager, Doug knew he needed to learn the computer's capabilities and have a good knowledge of its operation. He was soon doing the programming for WA. Doug and his wife Doris, WA artist, served for seven years, until mid-1976.

In every situation requiring divine guidance, when men rely on God, trust in his faithfulness, and wait for his time, he always shows the way. This was true as WA searched for a new president. Everyone was confident that God was preparing a person to fit the job.

Board member Bill Wyatt, another longtime supporter of Wycliffe and one of those who served on the committee that started WA, recommended Jim Shaner, a member of his church in Sacramento, California. Bill felt that Jim's experience in education, communications, and hospital administration had amply prepared him to lead Wycliffe Associates. For his part, Jim had "thought about" Christian work, but had always felt that if the Lord wanted him in a full-time Christian ministry, he would bring it about through a combination of circumstances. And God did.

"I was happy in hospital management," Jim says, "but as Bill described how WA was involving lay people directly in missionary work, something clicked in my mind, something saying: 'This is it. This is where I should be.' "

At Bill's urging Jim sent his resume to Rey Johnson, chairman of the search committee. The board was considering two other people at the time and it was more than a month before Jim and his wife Maxine were invited to Orange for interviews. The committee, well pleased, recommended Jim to the full board which, in turn, unanimously appointed him president of WA.

Jim responded, "I accept your offer. I have never felt so confident of the Lord's leading in my life." The combination of circumstances had fallen into place, one after the other.

Jim spent his first year at WA finding out who's who in Wycliffe, becoming familiar with Wycliffe structure and policy, and learning how WA relates to the overall Bible translation ministry. Travel took a large part of his time as he visited Wycliffe installations in the United States and South America, and WA area directors in their homes. Quarterly WA board meetings in various parts of the country enabled him to meet board members who live in other areas.

Working closely with U.S. Division Director Clarence Church, a gentle, competent administrator, Jim was able to get a comprehensive picture of WA's role as he and Clarence reviewed priorities and assigned projects.

At Jim's request, WBT vice-president for finance Jim Agnor began serving as WA's controller, spending several days a month in the Orange office.

"We exist solely to serve Wycliffe Bible Translators," the WA president stresses. "Thus we want to maintain a close liaison. We're not just an organization. We're Wycliffe's lay division with a specific, God-given function. Sometimes our efforts are directed toward the entire Wycliffe organization, sometimes toward a branch, and sometimes toward individuals, but always toward the end that God's Word may be translated into every language."

Jim is assisted by a dedicated staff, most of whom are lay people that God has led into the work of WA. Business manager Dale Herr and mail room supervisor Roger Petrey are engineers from the space industry; vice-president for construction Harold Leasure, field director for construction John Bender, and South America construction supervisor Wes Syverson had their own construction companies; vice-president for programs Warren Nelson, who has a background in architecture, was a pastor for eighteen years. Area directors Paul Chappell, Arthur Greenleaf, Stan Shaw, Ted Ulp, and David Houston are all laymen whose backgrounds have prepared them to carry on WA's field programs. A capable secretarial and bookkeeping staff rounds out the team.

The WA office headquarters are housed in a handsome new tiled-roof one-story structure at 202 South Prospect Avenue in Orange, California, about forty miles south of Los Angeles and a few minutes' drive from WBT's new headquarters in Huntington Beach. The building is small, but well equipped, and affords comfortable, pleasant surroundings for some twenty full-time employees. Complemented by a side yard of spreading evergreens, the attractive building blends tastefully into the residential neighborhood.

Most passing motorists who see the black WYCLIFFE ASSOCIATES logo flush against the outside wall probably think the building houses a law firm or a team of business consultants. The more discerning will notice the spear and twin shield emblem beside the name and the ham radio antenna towering above the roof. They may suspect that the building has a more unique purpose.

Inside the main reception room, offices branch off to left and right. In the mail room at the end of the hall, where Roger Petrey and his staff are sending out the WA *Newsletter*, Roger raises his voice over the competition of the postage machine that's stamping the day's first-class mail. An Apollo project engineer, Roger holds the Apollo Achievement Award. How does he feel about serving the Lord at WA?

"This is so much more satisfying than designing rockets to send space vehicles to the moon and beyond," he says, "because what I'm doing at WA to help reach Bibleless people has an eternal quality. Of the hundreds of pieces of mail we send out, some make contact with Christian people who'll respond to the needs of Bible translation in one way or another. I'm just one link in the chain of communication that ultimately results in producing the Scriptures in languages that weren't even written a few years ago. That means a lot more than helping to launch a space vehicle."

Often in devotions on Monday mornings, one can hear staff members expressing their thanks to God for calling them to serve him at WA. Each appreciates the abilities and expertise of the others—it is indeed a team—and each is grateful for the privilege of serving Wycliffe and the two hundred million people without God's Word in their languages.

"I'm so grateful to be part of this work," says the office redhead Sarah Pease. "Not only is it a joy and blessing to be working for the Lord, but in a small office like this, one is able to learn so many skills." Sarah has been at WA longer than any of the present staff and has done just about every job in the office. "I never wake up in the morning and dread to come to work," she smiles. "Instead, I praise God for my job and ministry and look forward to the day."

Receipting department director Carol Eldridge agrees. Carol loves the atmosphere of a Christian office and appreciates the fact that everyone in WA is striving toward a common purpose. "Our staff is only a small part of WA," she says. "There are WA members all over the world, all of whom are doing what they can where they are to help the cause of Bible translation."

The WA prayer closet means a lot to John Bender, who was WA's first construction field director in Porto Velho, Brazil. "We have a prayer schedule of fifteen-minute segments," John says. "Each day we can go into the prayer closet and remember one another, the missionaries on the field, the Bibleless people around the world, our donors and friends, the nations and governments with whom Wycliffe works, and any special requests we may have received from each other or from associates through the mail. It's really neat."

Area Director Stan Shaw and his wife Laurie, a part-time staffer, have a son with Wycliffe in Papua New Guinea. "The great thing about WA is that it provides a way for Christians to share in missionary work right where they are," says Stan. "I've met reservation secretaries who had no idea that calling people and inviting them to one of our dinner meetings could contribute anything to Bible translation. When we explained that it was through our dinner meetings that many people learned about Wycliffe for the first time, and that some were challenged to give and others to become translators, they were thrilled beyond words."

Working behind the scenes is the twenty-four-member board of trustees, most of whom are lay people, and all of whom are vitally interested in the work of Wycliffe and convinced that lay people are a strong link in the mission chain.

Several board members have relatives in WBT. WA's first woman board member, Mary Ann Mooney of Fullerton, California, is the sister of Bill Nyman, who has spent many years in Mexico and Colombia and is now on loan to Wycliffe Associates as director of member relations. Jim Henderson of Dearborn, Michigan, is the brother of European regional director Jack Henderson, and Bud Swanson is the father of Wycliffe member Kathie Watters, who serves with her husband John in Cameroon.

WA officers and executive committee are: Roger Tompkins, chairman; Harm te Velde, vice-chairman; Robert Seng, secretary; Billy Gibson, treasurer; Bud Swanson, Merlin Hoyt, and Bob Welch. All of the officers and executive committee are from Southern California except Bob Seng (Tucson, Arizona) and Billy Gibson (St. Simons Island, Georgia).

Even though the majority of WA board members live in other states, they are actively involved and, with quarterly meetings in various areas of the country, are able to contribute their experience and expertise to the ministry. Several have been on WA field assignments; many have visited the fields.

The other board members are: Lloyd Bontrager, Middlebury, Indiana; Ernest Comte, Tucson, Arizona; Harold Covey, Normal, Illinois; Linwood Erickson, Warren, Rhode Island; James Henderson, Dearborn, Michigan; Otto Janke, Palos Heights, Illinois; Bengt Junvik, Arcadia, California; Homer Kandel, Berlin, Ohio; Ed McAteer, Memphis, Tennessee; Charles Miller, Little Rock, Arkansas; Mary Ann Mooney, Fullerton, California; Rev. George Munzing, Santa Ana, California; Lawrence E. Olsen, Seymour, Illinois; Paul Von Tobel III, Valparaiso, Indiana; Dr. Ernest Warner, Edmond, Oklahoma; and R. W. "Bill" Wyatt, Sacramento, California. Each is successful in his respective profession.

Among the responsibilities of the WA board is the setting of policy within the articles of incorporation, developing plans and programs for advancement, approving the annual budget, and appointing the president, who is responsible to them for staff operations.

A major accomplishment of the WA board is the thirteen-story retirement facility, Wycliffe Plaza, in Santa Ana, California, completed in the fall of 1976. Concerned about Wycliffe missionaries in their later years, the board members felt something should be done to provide a place where they could retire after their active service with Wycliffe. "We don't believe we should help missionaries on the field and then forget about them when they retire and come home," says former chairman of the board Rey Johnson. "We're proud of Wycliffe Plaza and want to do more as the Lord opens the way."

Managed by associate Lee Farnsworth, Wycliffe Plaza is completely occupied and has a long waiting list.

The staff and board of WA continue to receive enthusiastic support from the organization they serve—Wycliffe Bible Translators. From his perspective, U.S. Division Director Clarence Church sees WA as being much more than a fund-raising organization. He believes WA has a more important function as a "friend raiser" for Wycliffe. Says Clarence, "They introduce fifteen to seventeen thousand new friends to Wycliffe every year. Their work is getting better and better."

And Wycliffe's chief executive officer Dr. Frank Robbins says, "WA is a vehicle for lay people to get involved with the task that drives us forward. Associates are coworkers with the translators. We're all in this work together. The only difference in WA and WBT is in the roles we play."

Perhaps Wycliffe's publication *In Other Words* has put it most succinctly:

> They [Wycliffe Associates] are doers ... Wherever they go, they leave in their wake a potpourri of things done. Missions accomplished. "We

came, we saw the need, we did something about it." Only, they wouldn't say it that way. They're not very good at tooting their own trumpets. But that's about the only place they fail. Impossible is not in their vocabulary.

All of these men and women—and even the children—are obsessed with a compulsion toward the goal of the Great Commission. They've become excited about missions on a tour, or as a member of a work party, or through a Wycliffe member or another "doer"—and they are really turned on. They come in all ages and from many races. Christ is their chief passion, the world their parish, and the Scriptures in every man's tongue their program. They are the Wycliffe Associates. And there's room for a few thousand more to join their ranks.